Martyred and Blessed Together

The Extraordinary Story of the Ulma Family

Fr. Paweł Rytel-Andrianik and Manuela Tulli

An interview with Cardinal Marcello Semeraro
in the Preface

Introduction by
Archbishop Stanisław Gądecki

Our Sunday Visitor
Huntington, Indiana

Scripture texts in this work are taken from the *New American Bible, revised edition* © 2010, 1991, 1986, 1970 Confraternity of Christian Doctrine, Washington, D.C., and are used by permission of the copyright owner. All rights reserved. No part of the *New American Bible* may be reproduced in any form without permission in writing from the copyright owner.

Every reasonable effort has been made to determine copyright holders of excerpted materials and to secure permissions as needed. If any copyrighted materials have been inadvertently used in this work without proper credit being given in one form or another, please notify Our Sunday Visitor in writing so that future printings of this work may be corrected accordingly.

Copyright © 2023 by Paweł Rytel Andrianik and Manuela Tulli

28 27 26 25 24 23   1 2 3 4 5 6 7 8 9

All rights reserved. With the exception of short excerpts for critical reviews, no part of this work may be reproduced or transmitted in any form or by any means whatsoever without permission from the publisher. For more information, visit: www.osv.com/permissions.

Our Sunday Visitor Publishing Division, Our Sunday Visitor, Inc., 200 Noll Plaza, Huntington, IN 46750; www.osv.com; 1-800-348-2440

ISBN: 978-1-63966-206-7 (Inventory No. T2899)
1. RELIGION—Christianity—Catholic.
2. HISTORY—Modern / 20th Century—Holocaust.
3. RELIGION—Christianity—Saints & Sainthood.
eISBN: 978-1-63966-207-4

Cover design: Tyler Ottinger

Interior design: Amanda Falk

Cover and interior art: Courtesy Ulma Family Museum

PRINTED IN THE UNITED STATES OF AMERICA

CONTENTS

PREFACE, *An Unprecedented Beatification*
    Interview with Cardinal Marcello Semeraro   7
INTRODUCTION, Archbishop Stanisław Gądecki   17

Chapter 1 — THE ULMA FAMILY, NEW MARTYRS   21
Chapter 2 — THE EIGHT JEWS KILLED
    WITH THE ULMAS   47
Chapter 3 — THE WAR   59
Chapter 4 — THE MASSACRE   85
Chapter 5 — RIGHTEOUS AND BLESSED   101

CONCLUSION   119
AFTERWORD (THE GENESIS OF A BOOK)   125
ACKNOWLEDGMENTS   129

APPENDIX I   131
APPENDIX II   145
NOTES   153
BIBLIOGRAPHY   165

"No one has greater love than this, to lay down one's life for one's friends." — *John 15:13*

PREFACE

An Unprecedented Beatification
An interview with Cardinal Marcello Semeraro
prefect of the Dicastery for the Causes of Saints

Has there ever been a beatification similar to that of the Ulma family? "In recent times and with the current procedures there have never been any; perhaps for such cases we need to go back to antiquity." This is the conclusion of the prefect of the Dicastery for the Causes of Saints, Cardinal Marcello Semeraro, who studied the Polish family's case and presented their story to Pope Francis to recommend their beatification.

Cardinal Semeraro hosted us in his offices on the third floor of the building that houses the dicastery, directly overlooking Saint Peter's Square. We are in a place that seems, somehow, between earth and heaven, surrounded by images of those who have experienced holiness in their everyday lives. Scattered on small tables are images of the most famous saints, of lesser-known ones, of priests, of nuns, but also of many laypeople, saints, and blesseds. Among them are also photos of the

Ulmas, "a lovely family," Semeraro says, smiling. "Their story moves me."

Your Eminence, is this the first time in the history of the Church that an entire family will be beatified together?

From the standpoint of current canonical procedure, it is a novelty, although there have been beatifications and canonizations of families in the history of the Church. But in the cases we have known up to the Ulmas, both the procedure for beatification and the beatification itself took place distinctly — that is, individually — following the principle that the first evaluation is on the exercise of the virtues in heroic form, an aspect that is unique and personal in one's life, although there are always relationships. There is a popular phrase: "No man is an island." And this, a fortiori, is true of holiness. The saints also live together, in the sense that in many cases saints meet each other and influence each other, we would say it is a kind of contagion, if this word did not have a negative connotation after COVID ... but that of the saints is a kind of positive contagion.

So the story of the Ulmas, who were martyred and beatified all together, both parents as well as the children, would be a unique case in the history of the Church.

Yes, indeed. There have not been any beatifications like this, not even in recent times and with current procedures. Families have been declared saints, but with individual canonizations. Think of the case of St. Thérèse of Lisieux's parents, Louis Martin and Azélie-Marie Guérin. They were proclaimed saints together,[1] but St. Thérèse had been canonized earlier. And in the case of the Ulmas, we are talking about martyrs. There were cases like this in antiquity, however, or similar situations; the [Roman] Martyrology mentions them. But for recent times this is a completely new thing, partially because of the procedure that was conducted for the whole family together. And this was so relevant to us in the dicastery that it encouraged us to promote a conference for reflection precisely on the "community dimension" of holiness — starting precisely from the case of the Ulma family.

It is as though the Ulma case has opened a new "track" in the history of saintliness.

In some ways, yes, because there is a whole family who suffered martyrdom; then the examination of their cause for beatification was conducted together; the decree was approved together; and together they are beatified.

Is it also novel that a child still in the womb, the Ulmas' seventh child, is considered a martyr by the Church?

This is an even newer situation. Both the Consultation of Theologians and the Ordinary Meeting of Cardinals and Bishops of the Dicastery, which then formulates the petition to the Holy Father, also included in the group a baby in the mother's womb, who probably initiated the delivery out of fear during the execution by the Nazis. This is a very unique case which, referring to a Gospel episode, we can call "Baptism of Blood." I am thinking of the Holy Innocents as a similar case.[2] Even this creature, whose head and part of the little body protruded from its mother's womb, as it was found in the mass grave in which the entire family had been hastily buried after the massacre, was deemed worthy of martyrdom.

In addition to the baby in the womb, there are the young siblings. Can one consider them martyrs? Marysia, the youngest, was one-and-a-half years old, and the others were a little older. It is possible they could not have consciously chosen martyrdom.

Martyrdom is never chosen; martyrdom is always endured as violence for the love of God. An ancient formula says that what makes the martyr is being killed in hatred of the Faith.

But maybe at that age they did not yet have full awareness of their faith.

They were Christians and were killed because a family, collectively, performed an act of charity. All nine Ulmas were Christians: It is that communal dimension of holiness that is unique to this case.

The procedure followed for beatification was that of martyrdom, but there is also talk of alleged miracles occurring through the Ulma family's intercession. Have you looked into them?

No. According to current ecclesiastical discipline, a miracle is not required for martyrdom. For a future canonization, however, a miracle would be needed.

A miracle is also required for the other type of beatification that has been instituted by Pope Francis — namely, the one referring to the "gift of life." In some respects, it is similar to martyrdom: It is the gift of self, but it is not actual martyrdom. There are already cases: In Italy there is one that can be examined from this perspective of the gift of life. It is the case of Salvo d'Acquisto.[3] But in the case of the gift of life, a miracle is required, and not necessarily the virtue that is referred to as "heroic." Although the word heroism — let me tell you — is dangerous today, it is misunderstood, because holiness is always the acceptance of a gift from God.

The Ulmas' home village of Markowa is about sixty kilometers from the Ukrainian border, less than an hour's drive. The Ukrainians are victims of war and hatred and the same history repeating itself. What can we do to not forget?

Prayer is what we hold most dear, it is always available, it is everything to us. There is a Latin phrase: *amor vincit omnia* (love conquers all). This beatification a few kilometers from the border of a war makes us think. ... But the pope always uses the expression of a world war in pieces — that is, it is everywhere. Although now, since there is this conflict in Ukraine, the pope — I think at the Sunday Angelus — always invokes prayer and uses the expression "the tormented Ukraine." But Pope Francis also reminds us of the many other hotbeds or conflicts all over the world. We are focused on this painful situation because it feels closer, but there are so many situations of violence and war everywhere.

There is an author, I do not remember the name, who says that we have lost the sacrificial spirit. In many cases, for painful situations like war, we have sent help, economic support, or military support; there is so much discussion about this even in Italy, and we believe we have done everything through material help. We feel at peace, and we no longer sense that ability to involve ourselves personally: the compassion, the suffering with others.

Compassion that the Ulmas, instead, felt and experienced by opening their doors ...

Yes, theirs is a true example of compassion; they risked their lives to house eight Jews for a year and a half. It is not just about helping; it is compassion that puts us in a position to suffer with the other person in order to help them. Emotional involvement is easy, but compassion is something else.

Let's talk now about your role as prefect of the Dicastery for the Causes of Saints. How do you present all these sto-

ries to the pope to then arrive at a decree that a person can be declared blessed or a saint?

I always give the pope a text that consists of three or four pages. At the beginning is the story, followed by the outcome of the investigation on our part, and finally the proposal that is made. The pope listens and then signs the decree. When the hearings are set, he knows that I have to bring him a certain number of decrees, and each one of them is a story. So far I have had as much time as is needed to present the different situations. In fact, sometimes the others, who had to speak to the Pontiff after me, have waited.

How did you present the story of the Ulmas to the pope?

I personally felt very invested in this story. This is a beautiful family, the husband and wife loved each other, within nine years they had six children and were expecting another. They were passionate about their work, farming, and they also had hobbies like photography and beekeeping. They are a very lovely family. Both of them had a Christian commitment. The wife attended church and was active in parish groups, and the husband was a highly spirited and well-known character in the village. A really nice family; this touched me and left me thinking a lot because of this communal dimension of holiness.

In your dialogue with Pope Francis, what aspect of the Ulmas' holiness stood out most?

With the pope, we talked about the two particularities of this beatification: the importance of the community dimension, that it is a whole family, and then the singularity of the children and of the baby that the mother was carrying and to whom, perhaps because of the terrible shock of that moment, began to give birth.

Finally, Your Eminence, out of curiosity, do you live better by being among the saints from morning to night?

I believe so. I can say that I have many stories that help me to be a good priest and a good Christian.

INTRODUCTION

I wish to thank the Holy Father for his decision to beatify Servants of God Józef and Wiktoria Ulma and their seven children. I thank the Holy See, especially Cardinal Marcello Semeraro and the entire Dicastery for the Causes of Saints, for all their hard work that has led to this important milestone. I am also grateful to Archbishop Adam Szal of the Diocese of Przemyśl for overseeing the diocesan phase of the beatification process.

The Jewish community in Poland has historically held great significance, not only because they were the country's largest minority before the Second World War but also because they are seen as our "elder brothers," as Pope St. John Paul II stated on April 13, 1986. Therefore, the beatification of an entire family for having helped Jews is momentous. "No one has greater love than this, to lay down one's life for one's friends" (Jn 15:13).

Let me quote from a letter sent by the Polish Bishops' Conference to churches throughout Poland:

> The life of the Venerable Servants of God Józef

and Wiktoria consisted of countless daily sacrifices and gestures of love. The fruit of adopting this way of life was the heroic decision to help Jews condemned to extermination. It was not a hasty decision but the result of reading the Word of God, which formed their hearts and minds and thus their attitude toward their neighbor. ... Józef and Wiktoria decided to take in eight Jews, despite the threat of death from the Germans for those who helped hide Jews. Three families took refuge in the attic of their small house: the Goldmans, the Grünfelds, and the Didners. For many months, they ensured them a roof and food, which, in wartime, is a real challenge.

Their attitude of self-sacrifice met its tragic end on March 24, 1944. Nazis broke into their home and cruelly shot the hiding Jews, and then, before the eyes of the children, they killed Józef and Wiktoria. To complete the tragedy, they killed the children. ... Their heroic attitude is a testimony that love is stronger than death.

Remarkably, all the children will be beatified along with their parents. A baby still in the womb, through the

Baptism of Blood, will also be beatified — something that has never happened before. I am grateful to Pope Francis because, with this gesture of beatifying an unborn baby, he offers hope to many parents whose children die in their mother's wombs or shortly after birth.

The museum in Markowa, whose inauguration I had the honor of participating in, reminds us of the Ulmas' example of Christian love and sacrifice, a sign of Christ's love that still touches us.

✠ Stanisław Gądecki
Metropolitan Archbishop of Poznań
President of the Polish Bishops' Conference

Chapter 1
THE ULMA FAMILY, NEW MARTYRS

The Ulmas were an ordinary family residing in Markowa, a village situated in the southeast of Poland, where the majority of the population were involved in agricultural work.[4] Józef and Wiktoria Ulma were busy raising their children, working, living Christian lives, and trying to help others as much as possible. They were a family blessed with many children — six in less than nine years of marriage, with a little one due to arrive in that tragic year of 1944, when they were wiped out by the murderous fury of the Nazis, along with their Jewish friends whom they had decided to host in their home.[5]

The Ulmas were an ordinary family whose life was peppered with the small joys of daily living, which Józef Ulma sought to capture in his photographs. He was in fact a great lover of, and even an expert in, photography, and this interest allows us today to enter their home and better understand their lives in the simplicity of the everyday.

In 1943, one year before the tragedy, Józef photographed one moment in his children's day. We see the oldest, Stasia, then seven years old, feeding Antoś, who is lying comically in the laundry basket. Next, Basia, Władziu, and Franio.

This was supposed to be one of many moments to frame or to put in the family album, but it turned instead into the iconic photograph of this heroic family. The photo has been edited to include Józef's portrait alongside his wife, Wiktoria, holding their young daughter Marysia and with their unborn child in her belly.

This remains the image of the Ulma family, whom everyone in Poland knows as the "Samaritans of Markowa."[6] According to Cardinal Konrad Krajewski, Pope Francis' almoner, the Ulma family "chose to protect life at the cost of their lives." The cardinal, who is often referred to as a modern-day Samaritan, highlights their unwavering commitment to the Gospel.

This small story of the Ulmas is woven into the broader story of Europe ravaged by the Second World War.

Józef

Józef Ulma was born on March 2, 1900, in Markowa. His parents, Marcin and Franciszka (née Kluz), were simple farmers. They owned three hectares (about seven and a half acres) of land and a small wooden house. One of Józef's brothers described their family life: "Our family was simple, with God-fearing parents and a mother who in the final years of her life attended Holy Mass every day. There were four of us siblings. Our parents prayed at home, we sang prayers dedicated to Our Lady, and each Sunday we went to Mass."[7] It was in this atmosphere of authentic Christian spirituality that Józef was also educated.

Józef Ulma (far right) with his parents and brothers (ca. 1934)

His parents enrolled little Józef in the local folk school ("folk schools" were residential schools established in rural areas), and he attended only four elementary school classes until 1911. He would later complete his education with agricultural courses. At 17, he became actively involved in the Catholic community and joined the Holy Mass Association of the Diocese of Przemyśl and the local Catholic Youth Association.

In 1921, it was time for Józef's military service, after which he enrolled in the Pilzno Agricultural School and graduated with outstanding results. Józef Ulma would become a pioneering farmer for his time. He was not content with traditional farming methods but introduced innovative solutions in fruit and vegetable growing, silkworm breeding, and beekeeping. He was a true pioneer in Poland in these last two sectors. His creativity and efforts were rewarded at the Przeworsk District Agricultural Exposition, organized by the local Agricultural Society in 1933. In particular, Józef was honored for "ingenious beehives of his own construction and design" and for "exemplary breeding of silkworms with their life tables." His silkworm breeding elicited the interest of his fellow villagers and Prince Andrzej Lubomirski of Przeworsk, who personally visited the Ulma farm to see Józef's innovations.

The Ulma Family, New Martyrs 25

Józef Ulma at his apiary. Some of the preserved beehives are now in the open-air museum in Markowa.

Józef Ulma had less than one hectare (about two and a half acres) of land to cultivate, but he managed to make the most of it with fruit-tree nurseries. The sale of seedlings became one of the sources of his family's livelihood. He is credited with introducing the first apple trees in Markowa that could bear fruit even in summers as a result of his experiments.

Like his agricultural activity, Józef's social engagements also grew. The 1930s were years of lively discussion and political development in the small village of Markowa. Józef willingly dialogued with members of the Peasant Party and the cooperative movement. These were the years when the first mutual-aid agencies were established in Poland. Józef was head of the Markowa Milk Producers' Cooperative for a time. He was also the Catholic Youth Circle librarian and president of the agricultural division in Przemyśl, among other positions.

He loved his community, that small village where all lived together, trying to support one another, especially in the challenging years Poland was experiencing because of the war that was now knocking on the country's door.

Based on the testimonies that have reached us, Józef indeed appears to have been a gifted individual, making the most of his skills as if he had taken the parable of the

The Ulma Family, New Martyrs **27**

Józef Ulma in the garden

talents from Matthew's Gospel literally.[8] There was, first of all, his passion for photography: He assembled his first camera himself, drawing on instructions he tracked down in books and specialized periodicals he had collected on the subject over the years. He then acquired more professional equipment and took many photos. He was the only photographer in the village, and thus everyone knew him for photography.

His archive remains one of the most vivid records of Markowa in those years. His photos tell the story of people's lives, their work in the fields, big and small events in Markowa and nearby villages, including first Communions, weddings, theatrical plays, and performances of the village orchestra. He also took photographs on commission, and his photos remain in private family collections in Markowa and vicinity.

Yet his most beautiful photographs, and by far the most numerous, are the private ones depicting his family, especially the children: playing in the fields, learning to write and draw at the kitchen table with their mother, Wiktoria, or attempting to pose for the family album. In those photos, the children are often laughing. Sometimes, they are neatly dressed, while at other times, their hair is messy. Still, they elicit great fondness even decades later, because above all, the serenity of that young family shines through.

Then there are the books. In addition to books on photography, the Ulma family's library contains volumes on a variety of subjects, such as electrical engineering, the use of wind on farms, radio engineering, nature, and technology. Józef's photography skills were widely recognized and in high demand throughout the region, but he also demonstrated his ingenuity in various other fields. He made, for example, equipment for binding books, a device for capturing radio waves, and a small electric windmill for charging batteries to store energy. As a result, the Ulmas were one of the first families in Markowa to replace kerosene lamps with electric ones.

On the shelves of that small house on the outskirts of the village, there are also some books that show the family's curiosity about the world, such as books on the wilderness of Australia, an atlas, and a dictionary of foreign terms. And, of course, there was the Bible, read, underlined, and lived.

Two distinct red lines are evident in the family Bible found at their home after the execution.

First, "For if you love those who love you, what recompense will you have?" from chapter 5 of Matthew's Gospel, the famous Sermon on the Mount, which states the duties of a Christian.

Second, the title of chapter 10 of the Gospel of Luke is underlined in red: "The Good Samaritan." And next to it is a note with a single word: "Yes." The parable tells of the man who helped another man attacked and wounded by robbers: The Samaritan, who belonged to a people who did not enjoy a good reputation, helped a man in distress without asking for anything in return, while others, a priest and a Levite, whom society considered more righteous, had passed him by, practicing that *in-*

Selected books from the library of Józef Ulma. Titles from many fields testify to his versatile interests.

The Ulma Family, New Martyrs 31

Using professional books and magazines, Józef Ulma built a camera, a radio, and even a small wind farm.

difference that kills, to use the words of Pope Francis.

The Good Samaritan serves as the prime example of Gospel solidarity. The Ulmas aimed to emulate this figure, emphasizing that phrase in their Bible with a red underline. They proved their ability to do the same, and even to go beyond the Good Samaritan's example, by sacrificing their lives to practice the charity they learned from the Gospel. For these reasons, the Ulmas are now commonly called "the Samaritans of Markowa."

Another book of spirituality found in the house of the Ulma family was the life of Saint Josaphat, a Greek Catholic who lived between 1580 and 1623 in the same eastern part of Europe and is venerated as a martyr in the Catholic Church. We can infer from this that Józef and Wiktoria admired particularly those who were capable of sacrificing their lives for the sake of total fidelity to Jesus Christ.

Wiktoria

Wiktoria Niemczak was also born in Markowa, on December 10, 1912. She was the seventh child of Jan Niemczak and Franciszka Homa. She lost her mother prematurely when she was only six years old. Her grandmother raised her for some time; then her father found a new wife, a second mother for Wiktoria. Jan would die one year before Wiktoria's marriage to Józef Ulma.

There was a rule in the Niemczak family: No one who came to them for help could leave the house without having something done for them. This sensitivity and attention to the needs of others, learned during those years of living in her family of origin, would stay with Wiktoria until her death.

Wiktoria attended the folk school, obtaining good grades, including one for the study of the German language. Then she took courses at the People's University in Gać. If Józef was passionate about technology, his future wife was more of an artist. She drew and acted. In particular, she performed in the parish theater, portraying Our Lady at a Christmas celebration. It was possibly through the parish amateur theater group that Wiktoria met her future husband.

Wiktoria seems to have been a reserved person who gave priority to her home and family. Compared with her husband, who was well known in the village through his numerous activities, we have fewer detailed accounts of her in testimonies from that time. But from the many photographs of Wiktoria, we can infer that she was the linchpin of the family, the rock on which the daily structure rested.

Józef portrayed her with the children, alone, in poses with him, and even in tender embraces. When the young woman was doing everyday tasks like making a snack for her children, assisting them with their homework, arranging a picnic, or comforting one of her crying daughters, there was a special sparkle in her eyes.

Wiktoria had an innate elegance, even though she wore clothes for work or representing everyday life at home. She had close-cropped hair and, above all, the serene eyes of a woman who knows that her mission is to support her family, stand by her husband, and raise the many children who arrived over just a few years.

Her friends spoke of her as a sunny and welcoming person. Among them was Stanisława Kuźniar, the godmother of Władziu, the Ulmas's third son. Stanisława is also depicted in one of Józef's photographs, holding little Władziu's hand. She was then in her twenties and was close friends with this family; she would be the last surviving witness during the beatification process and offered valuable details and information since she had known Józef and Wiktoria personally.

Stanisława spoke of her friendship with Wiktoria, to whom she was also related: "My mother died when I was four. After her death, my father married Maria, Wiktoria's sister."[9] Stanisława was a frequent guest at Józef's and Wiktoria's home. She helped her friend with household chores and cared for the children, especially when Wiktoria had to rest after giving birth to another child. All of the births took place in that small house with one common room, and Wiktoria dealt with the pains of labor shielded only by a curtain.

Speaking of Wiktoria, in the testimony given to the Przemyśl diocesan office as part of the inquiry opened for beatification, Stanisława said that "she was a good, warm, and friendly woman."[10] The two friends, close even in age and, in fact, like sisters, understood each other very well, and they supported each other.

Józef was devoted to his wife, and when he had to make important decisions, he did not do it alone but always consulted her first. Witnesses from that time recounted that it was as if he were walking a step behind her — not something one might expect, perhaps, from a man who was one of the best-known, and even the most respected, people in the village of Markowa.

Speaking of the moment when the couple decided to take eight Jews into their home, putting their lives and those of their children in danger, the postulator of the family's cause for beatification, Fr. Witold Burda, highlights Wiktoria's essential role. "As postulator, and by reading different testimonies and diverse material concerning their lives, I am convinced that both spouses, Józef and Wiktoria, made this decision together. It was not Józef alone."[11]

The writer Maria Elżbieta Szulikowska dedicated a book to this woman: *Wiktoria Ulma: A Love Story*.[12] After a pilgrimage to the Ulmas' grave, she had written a poem about the family, which later became a song. But she felt the need to tell more about the young woman and, above all, about her Christian faith. "Her bright gaze could make feminists green with envy,"[13] says the writer, speaking of Wiktoria's boundless maternal love that cannot but be linked to her love for Christ.

"I wrote this book because so much attention in various publications is devoted to her husband, Józef, photographer, fruit grower, and social activist. And Wiktoria remained in the shadows, even though she had six children and a whole house to care for," Szulikowska says. "So, I wanted to show the world a mother who, after all, is a candidate for beatification. Once, as I was enlarging a photograph of her on the computer screen, I saw a twinkle in her eyes. Her secret of happiness fascinated me." She also recalls the words of a great love that Wiktoria would repeat when talking about her children: "*Children are like flowers. They need a lot of love, wisdom, attention, and proper care.*"

Her role in the family, then, was anything but secondary for the young woman who, at the age of 31, already had seven children when she met a heinous death at the hands of the Nazis. Her legacy, rather than being material (we have no photographs or tools of her work, as we do of Józef), is this love that spread to her entire family and even to her friends.

Marriage and Children

Józef and Wiktoria were married on July 7, 1935, in St. Dorothy parish church in Markowa. Józef was 35 years old, and Wiktoria twelve years younger — a fairly common age difference back then. Dozens of people attended their wedding feast, which is documented in a photo of that day. Józef is wearing a dark suit jacket and pants with a white shirt underneath; in his breast pocket is a flashy white handkerchief, which looks more like a bow. His hair and mustache are well groomed for the big occasion. Wiktoria is wearing a traditional white wedding dress with a veil and a small crown on her head to hold her hairstyle in place. Next to them, the men are dressed in elegant, festive suits, while the women and girls are wearing traditional Polish costumes with embroidered bodices and necklaces with several strands of pearls covered with floral fabric flowing down their chests. A few children are dressed as sailors. Seated on the ground

38 *Chapter 1*

Wedding of Wiktoria and Józef Ulma, July 7, 1935

in front of the large group of guests are the members of the little musical orchestra that, with its Pianola, trumpet, and drum, brightened the festive day.

Józef and Wiktoria's wedding was anything but an event celebrated with just a few close friends and relatives. Dozens and dozens of people are squeezed close together in the photograph. Józef is looking right into the camera lens and smiling. Wiktoria's gaze is more serious, but we do not know if that is from excitement or the fatigue that wedding preparations always entail, or simply because she was less accustomed than her husband to the medium of a camera, which captured the moments of everyday life and returned them as images much more realistic than her drawings, in which she tried to capture the landscapes surrounding her life and the lives of her dear ones.

Józef was busy cultivating and tending their land, working in a dairy, and engaging in social life. Wiktoria, in turn, cared for their home and their large family. There must have been so many daily tasks and household chores to be borne by such a young woman with so many young children to raise and care for.

Things were all right financially, but the family was growing rapidly. For this reason, Józef and Wiktoria decided in 1938 to invest in a five-hectare (a little over twelve acres) plot of land in Sokal (a town now located in Ukraine, in the Lviv area, on the border with Poland), to which the family would move. Despite their attachment to the village of Markowa in which they were both born and raised, they thought that to offer their children a better future they had to move and expand their farming business. Because of the outbreak of World War II, this dream would never come true.

Józef and Wiktoria loved each other. One photo shows them embracing; she is sitting on her husband's lap as he is lovingly holding her — a pose that was perhaps even a little bold given the sense of modesty that then prevailed in society when it came to couples. That love between Józef and Wiktoria was also fueled by a common Christian faith lived with simplicity in everyday life — praying, reading the Gospel, attending Mass, and participating in Church activities. The genuine faith they had both breathed as children in their respective families they were now committed to passing on to their children.

Their first child, Stasia, arrived almost exactly one year after their marriage: She was born July 18, 1936. At the time of her death in 1944, she was preparing for her first Communion and was not yet eight years old. Her brothers and sisters soon followed, almost one per year: Basia on October 6, 1937; Władziu on December 5, 1938; Franio on April 3, 1940; Antoś on June 6, 1941; and little Marysia, born September 16, 1942, who was only a year and a half old at the time of the massacre.

Józef and Wiktoria had already taught the young children the Sign of the Cross and their first prayers. Father Burda relates one of the testimonies collected during the cause of beatification. "Józef and Wiktoria — according to the account of one of the witnesses at the time — were good people; they were a very close couple, and they loved their children very much," is re-

The Ulma Family, New Martyrs **41**

In front of the Ulma house after Antoś's christening (summer 1941). From left: Władysław Ulma with Władz, the midwife named Szpytma, godparents – Maria Niemczyk holding the baptized Antoś and Antoni Ulma, Katarzyna Ulma, Wiktoria Ulma with her son Frank and before her Basia, Marcin Ulma (Józef's father) with Stasia.

counted. "I lived for a week in their house after Wiktoria had given birth to their third child. I remember that the children were very polite. Józef would kneel with them in the evening to pray,"[14] while Wiktoria was in bed recovering from childbirth.

Thanks to the photographs, we also have a reasonably accurate idea of what their house looked like. (It is no longer there today.) It was a country cottage a few hundred meters from the main road, with two rooms downstairs and an attic. This small, neat, cozy house

The house of the Ulma family, built by Józef in the 1930s, a wooden structure with a gable roof covered with tiles.

welcomed family members and anyone in need. Everyone knew that the Ulmas' home was always open to them. The pictures captured by Józef depict a household overflowing with love, kindness, and warmth.

The Ulma's marriage was very harmonious: "They loved each other and treated each other with great respect," recounted their friend and relative Stanisława Kuźniar. Theirs was a home and a family in which, despite the commotion of many small children and occasional difficulties because of their modest living conditions, there was never a moment of anger; "there was no shouting or swearing or even a raised voice. … There was only joy and harmony in that home."

The couple loved their children very much and based their education on good example and kindness. They hardly needed to scold them. And thus, Stanisława recounts further "those children were always joyful and well behaved; they were not afraid of people; they were open and trusted everyone."[15]

The Ulmas had many friends, and their home was constantly bustling. They had a relationship of trust and esteem with their neighbors, which is perhaps why they did not take too many precautions when they decided to house Jewish families, despite the risk of the death penalty imposed by the Nazis.

Their relationship with the Jews who lived in Markowa was also very good, even before World War II began. Some Jewish families lived right next door to the Ulmas. Józef traded with them the vegetables he grew and sold to them the leather he had learned to tan in a small corner of the house that served as his workshop. Based on these relationships, it was, therefore, a natural decision to help them when they were in danger during the Nazi persecution.

In their modest two-room house, the Ulmas provided shelter for three Jewish families: the Goldmans, the Grünfelds, and the Didners. To these eight people,

Józef and Wiktoria Ulma soon after their wedding (around 1936)

wanted by the Germans, the Ulmas offered a hiding place in their attic for over a year. They also helped four other Jewish women. Józef prepared a hiding place for them, and Wiktoria regularly brought them food. Unfortunately, the women did not survive the Holocaust.

Making a choice, as the Ulmas did, based on faith and in the pursuit of peace seemed nearly impossible during the dark days of the war. "This martyred family is a hymn to peace," said Bishop Giuliano Brugnotto of the Diocese of Vincenza, Italy, in his 2022 Christmas greeting addressing the families of his diocese. "They did not react to violence with more violence. They reacted to the brutality of war with the generosity of hospitality. When you truly love, you risk your life."[16]

Chapter 2
THE EIGHT JEWS KILLED WITH THE ULMAS

Different families hid the Jews in Markowa, but the largest group of eight people found refuge in the Ulma home, probably in December 1942. They included Saul Goldman with his adult sons Baruch, Mechel, Joachim, and Moses. The Goldmans were from the nearby town of Łańcut, where they were known as the Szalls. Then there were two sisters (daughters of Chaim Goldman, a relative of Saul's), Gołda Grünfeld and Lea (Layka) Didner. The latter also had a small daughter named Reszla with her. It seems that these families asked the Ulmas for help after the great massacre of Jews that had taken place in Markowa earlier in 1942.

The Goldmans

The Goldman family was one of the earliest known Jewish families in Markowa and bore one of the most popular Jewish surnames in the area.[17] The family's progenitor was Baruch (born around 1835), from whom Saul Goldman and his sons descend.

Baruch Goldman had four children from his first marriage with Fajga Ethel: Mechel, Wolf (Szlomo Zev), Gołda, and Lea. After his wife's death, Baruch remarried Reśla Miller, with whom he had seven children: Chaim (called the eldest), Mordechaj, Jakub, Itta, Mania, Joel, and Chana.[18]

His eldest son from his first marriage, Mechel (born around 1857), moved to Hadle Kańczuckie, about twelve kilometers from Markowa. There he became involved with Chana Resengarten (born around 1852), with whom he had six children. Their eldest child, named Fajga Ettel after her grandmother, died shortly after her birth in 1880. Their first son, Chaim Nuchem, was born in 1881. Saul (who later lived with his children with the Ulma family) entered the world in 1883 in Hadle Kańczuckie. Later, the family moved to Kraczkowa, where Beil (1886) and Berel (1888) were born. Markus was born in 1889; by then the family was already living in Markowa. Because Mechel and Chana did not legalize their union for a long time, their children bore their mother's name, Rosengarten.[19]

The Goldmans cutting and chopping firewood on the Ulma property, where they were hiding. They worked for a joint livelihood, which is documented by a photo taken by Józef Ulma. All of them were shot along with the other inhabitants of the house on March 24, 1944.

Mechel's eldest son, Chaim Nuchem, moved to Krasne, near Rzeszów. He married Ita Rosenbaum (who was from that village) in 1910; the newlyweds moved to the city of Rzeszów. Their son was born there in 1912 and named Boruch after his grandfather. Chaim, as the eldest son, took care of his parents. In 1912, he brought his parents to live with them in the city. His father, Mechel, died one year later, in 1913, and his mother, Chana, died in 1929.

Mechel's and Chana's second son, Saul, married

Gołda Sauer and moved from Markowa to Łańcut, his wife's place of origin.[20] The Sauer family was well known and engaged in the cattle and butcher trade. Gołda's father, Abe, was one of the prominent representatives of Orthodox Jews in discussions with local Zionists. The family's mindset is reflected in the fact that Abe Sauer was one of the signatories of a letter that said:

> We Orthodox are Jews but Polish by tradition. We are Jews because we profess the Jewish religion. Still, we do not mix religion with politics, and with foreign Jews, we are concerned only with confessional bonds. In politics, we are Poles, submissive to the Polish state, serving only the orders of law and state.[21]

Saul's and Gołda's four children received their education in this home and intellectual environment. Their firstborn son, born in 1911, was named after his great-grandfather Baruch. Their second son, born in 1914, was named Mechel, after his grandfather, who had died a year earlier in Rzeszów.

Joachim was born in 1919, and Moses Fejwel was born in 1921. Saul lived with his family in Łańcut at No. 21 of the street that in the 1920s was dedicated to President Ignacy Mościcki of Poland. Neighbors called them the Szall family after their father's name, Saul. Before his father's passing, Saul went by his mother's surname, Rosengarten. However, after his father's death, he started using the surname Goldman.[22]

Sometime before 1929, Saul took over the slaughterhouse that had belonged to his father-in-law. He bought cattle for slaughter in the villages around Łańcut, including Markowa, his father's home village. We know that Józef Ulma already had a relationship with him because he tanned leather for his family. It was one of the many economic activities the Ulmas did to earn a living to support their large family.

Saul Goldman's brother, Markus Rosengarten (Goldman),[23] was the first Markowa victim of the Nazis. This is how Kamil Kopera, a researcher on the fate of the Jews of Markowa, describes him:

> It is not known when exactly [Markus] emigrated from his homeland, went to Vienna, and married. He obtained citizenship in Austria. He witnessed the growing terror of the Nazi regime. After March 12, 1938, Austria came under the control of Nazi Germany, and the Jews living there fell victim to its policies. On the night of

November 9–10, 1938, synagogues in the Third Reich were burned, Jewish cemeteries were desecrated, and the streets were covered with fragments of broken windows of Jewish homes and stores. This so-called Kristallnacht was an organized and targeted action against Jews living in the country, followed by mass arrests and deportations. More than 30,000 Jews ended up in concentration camps, of whom 11,000 were sent to Dachau Concentration Camp. Among them were many Viennese Jews, including Markus Rosengarten, who was arrested in his apartment at Reichsbrückstrasse 8. He arrived at Dachau on November 14, where he was given the number 25087. The register states that he was there as an Austrian Jew under "protective custody." He survived a few months in the harsh conditions of the camp. Although the Nazi authorities gradually liberated the camps, letting the inmates go, Markus did not live to see his release — he died on January 21, 1939, in Dachau.[24]

Kamil Kopera believes that

information about his brother's fate most likely reached Saul and influenced his decision to flee the Germans. Probably still, in September 1939, he went to the eastern territories already occupied by the USSR, with many Jews from Łańcut and the surrounding area. In late 1939, Abe, Gołda's father, who was over seventy years old, moved into the house at 21 Mościckiego Street. Saul Goldman returned to his family in 1941 after the outbreak of war between the Third Reich and the USSR. In the Jarosław district, which included Łańcut, the Germans carried out a deportation action on August 1, 1942. Saul's wife hid with her brothers' families in the city's center. She was killed after German gendarme Josef Kokott had discovered her hiding place.[25]

Saul's sons knew that Mechel worked as a dental technician for Antoni Białowicz in Łańcut, and then, as he wrote, was "a regular dental assistant in Lviv"[26] where he fled with his paternal brothers for fear of the Nazis. During World War II, he served as a doctor in the Polish army in 1939.

At first, the Goldmans found a hiding place with Włodzimierz Leś. This is how Mateusz Szpytma, a historian from Markowa, describes their experience:

> [The Goldmans,] realizing the approach of the so-called final solution, began to seek refuge. Włodzimierz Leś, a police officer from Łańcut, promised it to them. Leś lived in the suburbs of Łańcut, not far from the Goldmans, with whom he maintained close contact before the war. He then helped them go into hiding in exchange for material benefits.
>
> We can infer that when he realized that the Germans not only threatened to kill those who helped Jews but also carried out that penalty, the Goldmans had to look for another hiding place. However, they constantly asked Leś for help with the part of their property that remained in his hands, but to no avail. So, they tried to reclaim their property — to take it back or receive other property from Leś's estate in exchange. Preserved documents of the underground People's Security Guard suggest that fearing the loss of his Jewish property, Leś betrayed the Goldmans' hideout to his colleagues in the German gendarmerie.[27]

The Goldmans hid in the Ulmas's house together with their sisters Gołda and Lea, and Lea's daughter, Reszla.

Gołda Grünfeld and Lea Didner

The parents of Lea and Gołda (the two sisters hosted by the Ulmas) were Chaim and Estera (Ettel) Goldman, some of the wealthiest Jews in Markowa. Since no records survived, it is unclear if they were related to Baruch Goldman, although their surname would suggest so.

Chaim married Ester (Ettel) Riesenbach in 1907 in Łańcut. She was the daughter of Izaak and Lajla Landau, who, in the nearby village of Gać, were in the alcoholic beverage trade.

Chaim Hersh and Ester Goldman were farmers. They were landowners (with a multi-hectare farm) and merchants; they ran a store in the village, right at the intersection of the main street, where the roads to Łańcut, Kańczuga, and Przeworsk started. The store's location was strategic, and, as a result, it generated significant profits. That is how they became the wealthiest Jewish family in Markowa.

In their Markowa home at No. 783, seven children were born: Lea (Lyka, born in 1907, who later went into hiding with the Ulma family); Rifka (1908); Baruch

(1910, who died after two months); Jakub (1911); Gołda (1913, who also later went into hiding with the Ulma family); Chana (1916), and Matylda (1918).

In 1932, Lea briefly left Markowa and married Abraham Selman Didner of Głogów. They lived in Zabajka and Głogów. Their son, Becael Jehuda, was born in 1934. By then, the couple was already living in Markowa, where two younger sons were born: Izaak Hersch (1936) and Reiszel (1938).

In 1935, Gołda married Feivel Grünfeld, four years her senior. He came from the nearby village of Rokietnica, where he was a farmer. On August 27, 1937, at Gołda's family home in Markowa No. 783, their daughter Reiszel was born.

The other two daughters of Chaim and Ester Goldman, Chana and Matylda, who were still little at the outbreak of the war and the persecution of the Jews by the Nazi, remained with their parents in the family house near Zabratówka. They all probably hid in the nearby towns during the period of greatest danger, but they did not survive the Holocaust.[28]

The Jews hiding in the Ulma family's home might have contributed economically to their upkeep, because they stayed for over a year. However, we know that they did not have much money. The Szalls, the largest group in hiding (five people, a father with four sons), had previously sold their property to pay a person who promised to help but did not keep his commitment. That person, as mentioned earlier, was Włodzimierz Leś, who later allegedly spied for the Nazis. It was Leś who decided on the control operation at the Ulma house, leading to the subsequent killing of everyone there.

Włodzimierz Leś was a member of the "blue" Łańcut police, so called because of the color of their uniforms. The Blue Police, established in occupied Poland, were subordinate to the German security forces. According to later investigations, Leś was a collaborator with the German occupiers. Some considered him a Ukrainian because of his Greek Catholic faith.[29]

While the Szalls had little wealth, the daughters of the wealthy Chaim Goldman had more possessions. Gołda Grünfeld still possessed her gold jewelry at the time of her execution. The German gendarmerie found and stole it after the killing. That seems to be evidence that the Ulmas did not ask for valuables in exchange for their hospitality beyond perhaps some small contributions to meet everyday needs.

Despite the cramped quarters of the Ulma house, which was too small for the family itself, the Ulmas and the Jewish families they hid lived together peacefully for about a year and a half. But eventually, the large quantities of food that Wiktoria purchased attracted the attention of neighbors.

The suspicion that there must be more people in the house began to circulate in the village. Some believed that the food supplies Wiktoria bought were too much for the couple and their children. Passers-by reported seeing strangers near the Ulmas's house, even though it was a few hundred meters from the main road.

Once, Stanisława, Wiktoria's friend, noticed a man working on leather behind the house, as she would later recount. Yet she thought nothing of it, assuming he was a worker, and she did not ask her friends about his presence, either. However, neighbors or others may have realized, as the months went by, that some people were staying in the Polish family's house.

In addition to the Jewish families who stayed with them, there were four other Jewish women whom the Ulma family helped. Józef Ulma prepared a hiding place for them, and Wiktoria regularly brought them food. Unfortunately, the women were found during a chase on December 13, 1942, and shot the next day by the Germans.[30]

Chapter 3
THE WAR

To understand what the Ulma family and the Jews they hid experienced, we need to look at the circumstances under which they lived.

For 700 years, the largest number of Jews in the world lived in Poland.[31] The well-known Jewish historian Antony Polonsky writes: "By the mid-seventeenth century the Jewish community of Poland-Lithuania was the largest in Ashkenaz. A century later it was the largest Jewish community in the world with a population of over three-quarters of a million, and probably made up more than a third of world Jewry."[32]

In fact, during the Middle Ages, when they were deprived of their rights in Western European countries and had to emigrate, Jews found better living conditions in Poland.[33] One example of this is the set of privileges granted to Jews by King Casimir the Great (1310–70). From the fourteenth to the eighteenth centuries, Jews in Kraków lived in the neighborhood of Kazimierz, which in time became a district of the city and was named in memory of that king. Interestingly, even in Markowa, the district where most Jews lived was called Kazimierz.[34]

One of the legends about the arrival of Jews in Poland claims that Poland's name has its roots in the Hebrew *Polin*. Shmuel Yosef Agnon, a prominent Jewish writer and winner of the Nobel Prize for Literature in 1966, recounts that legend this way:

> When they arrived from the land of the Franks, they found a forest in Poland where a Talmudic treatise was engraved on every tree. It was the forest of Kawęczyn, on the road to Lublin. And behold, they believed that from the name of this country flowed a holy spring: the word of the people of Israel. And they said, *po lin*, which means, "Rest here." This is where we want to rest until God allows us to return to the land of Israel.[35]

For centuries Poland was a multiethnic country, and Jews were the largest national minority. In 1931, there were 3.1 million Jews in Poland — about 10 percent of the population. Moreover, Jews were the most active and diverse national community. The Jewish community had a vibrant religious, artistic, cultural, media, and even political life. The largest number of Jews were located in eastern Poland in the small towns called *shtetl* in Yiddish, where they made up half or more of the population. They were mainly engaged in trade and crafts, especially tailoring and shoemaking. They were also active in the food industry.

After Poland regained independence in 1918, a constitution was adopted in March 1921 guaranteeing citizens protection of life, liberty, and property, regardless of origin, nationality, language, race, or religion. The constitution guaranteed freedom of speech, press, and association. It also abolished the laws left in Poland by the country's partitioners (Russia, Prussia, and Austria). In 1931, the Polish Parliament (Sejm) passed a law abolishing provisions restricting citizens' rights "on the grounds of origin, nationality, language, race, or religion."

After the death in 1935 of Marshal Józef Piłsudski, who effectively ruled the Polish state, there was a growth of anti-Semitism in Poland. One way this manifested was in the boycott of Jewish goods and services. There were also demonstrations and pamphlets asking people not to purchase from Jewish stores, as well as destruction of Jewish property. Unfortunately, at that time, the rise of anti-Semitism was seen in many European countries, and in Germany anti-Semitism was institutionalized. By 1935, the so-called Nuremberg Laws had been adopted, depriving those of Jewish nationality of their public rights, including the right to vote. They could also be stripped of their citizenship.[36]

Outbreak of Second World War

No other country during World War II was so subjugated by Germany for so long a time, and in so devastating a way, in terms of the destruction of population and material goods, as was Poland.[37] For more than five years, Nazis treated Poland as a testing ground for mass genocide, terror, and the looting of goods.

At dawn on September 1, 1939, Germany, without declaring war, crossed the Polish border. At 4:40 a.m., the German air force began bombing Wieluń. The city, which had no military presence to defend it, was practically taken by surprise while the population slept.

More than 1,200 people were killed, and 90 percent of the city center was destroyed. This attack marked the beginning of military operations in World War II and occurred five minutes before the bombing of Westerplatte. At 4:45 a.m., the German warship Schleswig-Holstein opened fire on the Westerplatte peninsula outpost in Danzig, where about two hundred soldiers were manning the camp. Thus began World War II.

On September 17, 1939, the Soviet Union in turn invaded Poland, attacking it from the east. The next day, Polish President Ignacy Mościcki and Commander-in-Chief Edward Rydz-Śmigły left Poland for Romania, where both were interned. On September 28, the capital city of Warsaw was captured.

In October, the Germans divided the occupied territories of Poland. Areas bordering Germany that belonged to Germany before World War I and those that were economically valuable were incorporated into the Third Reich. In other areas, with the exception of Poland's eastern territories that had been taken on September 17 by the Soviet Union, the Germans created the so-called General Governorate, headed by Hans Frank, a resident of Kraków.

The German plan was for the territories incorporated into the Third Reich to be completely Germanized; Poles and Jews were regarded as "foreign elements" to be "removed."[38] The Governorate General was to be a reservoir of "subhumans" who would serve Germany as a cheap labor force.

In the Governorate General there were about 12.3 million people, of whom over ten million were Poles and 2,248,000 were Jews (by German calculations).[39] In a speech made on December 16, 1941, Governor General Hans Frank stated, "We must destroy the Jews wherever we find them and wherever possible in order to maintain the entire structure of the Reich."[40]

In the territories they occupied, the Soviets carried out ethnic cleansing. They transported people from those territories deep into the Soviet Union, particularly to Siberia and Kazakhstan. Among those deported were Poles and Jews. And they likewise transferred people from the depths of the Soviet Union to the occupied territories within the borders of Poland.

To achieve their goals, the Germans abolished Polish education and the Polish press. Intellectuals were often sent to prisons and labor camps. The occupied territories were quickly turned into a police state.

Endlösung (The Final Solution)

The beginning of World War II marked the start of an especially tragic period for the Jewish people, as well as the Roma and Sinti people, throughout Europe. The Nazis' plan was carried out in stages. One of the first German regulations dealt specifically with Jews.[41]

As early as September 21, 1939, Reinhard Heydrich, one of the chief murderers of the Jewish people during the Holocaust, sent a secret recommendation to German commanders in the occupied territories.[42] He ordered the liquidation of small concentrations (less than five hundred people) of the Jewish population and their concentration in ghettos in order to impose the so-called Final Solution (Endlösung). He also ordered the creation of "councils of elders" consisting of Jews, who were to be forced by the Germans to carry out their orders.[43]

During the first months of the war, the Germans also introduced certain racial laws in the territories of occupied Poland. Jews had to wear a yellow Star of David on their clothing, to make them easier to be identified; they could not use public transportation and could not leave their homes without specific permission. Their assets, stores, businesses, and workshops were confiscated. The German occupiers burned down many synagogues and Jewish libraries, including the famous Chachmei Lublin Yeshiva library.[44]

From the beginning of the war, the Germans created ghettos to isolate Jews from the rest of the population. The first ghetto in occupied Poland was established in October 1939 in Piotrków Trybunalski. This was publicly explained as necessary to protect the other inhabitants from infectious diseases. At the entrances to the ghettos or neighborhoods where Jews lived, the occupiers placed signs in Polish and German that read, "Area at risk of typhus." The Germans created more than five hundred ghettos for Jews in occupied Poland. The largest one was in Warsaw; at one point it reached nearly half a million people, who were crowded into a very small space. From the ghettos, Jews were deported to death camps or shot outside the cities, especially in eastern Poland.[45]

In mid-1941, German troops occupied the eastern territories of Poland, from which the Soviets had withdrawn. Along with the army, came special German units (Einsatzgruppen) who were the ones who shot Jews in the newly occupied territories. The crimes at Babi Yar near Kyiv or Ponary near Vilnius are examples of such killings.[46]

On October 15, 1941, Governor General Hans Frank issued a decree that Jews who left their designated district (ghetto) were subject to the death penalty.[47]

Similarly, Poles who hid and helped the Jewish population were threatened with the death penalty. Jews who escaped from the ghetto were often executed where they were discovered. Poles who rescued Jews were murdered in public places in the center of the city to deter others from helping the Jewish population.

On January 20, 1942, a conference of the highest officials of the Third Reich, chaired by Heydrich, took place in Wannsee near Berlin.[48] Those officials decided on the "final solution to the Jewish question" (Endlösung der Judenfrage), the genocide of the Jews throughout Europe.

On the night of March 16–17, 1942, German forces began "Operation Reinhard," the "liquidation" of the Lublin Ghetto. The purpose of this action was to kill nearly two million Jews in the General Governorate. The command, located in Lublin, was led by Odilo Globocnik, one of the chief murderers of Jews during the Holocaust.

Concentration Camps

A network of concentration and extermination camps was established in the territories of occupied Poland.[49] As early as 1939, the Stutthof concentration camp near Danzig was established. In 1940, the Auschwitz concentration camp was established. The first mass transports of victims arrived there on June 14, 1940. There were Poles in the first transports, but soon it would be mostly specifically Jews who were brought there. In 1941, the Majdanek concentration camp was opened. Over time, these camps also became places of mass extermination of Jews. From December 8, 1941, an extermination camp at Kulmhof also operated in Wartheland.[50]

Some of the camps that later became extermination sites were initially labor camps. Treblinka I was a penal labor camp organized for Poles as early as the late summer of 1941, although it was officially established on November 15, 1941.[51] Bełżec was also initially a complex of labor camps for Jews.

Under Operation Reinhard, three camps were established or expanded: Bełżec, Sobibór, and Treblinka.[52]

The first mass transports of Jews to the death camps under Operation Reinhard left the Lublin ghetto on March 17, 1942, for the Bełżec death camp. The Sobibór camp began operations in May 1942. The first transport of Jews from the Warsaw ghetto to the Treblinka II camp left on July 22, 1942.

The Nazis sent not only Jews from Polish ghettos but also from many other parts of Europe to the extermination camps in occupied Poland. The decision was made to establish these camps in the territories of occupied Poland because Poland had the largest population of Jews.

The Nazis used the railway lines to transport victims to the camps. Operation Reinhard officially lasted until November 3–4, 1943. The so-called Operation

Harvest Festival (Aktion Erntefest) took place on those days. Then the Nazis killed 42,000 people, including about 18,000 Jewish prisoners in the Majdanek concentration camp on the outskirts of Lublin.[53]

It is estimated that nearly two million Polish Jews were killed during Operation Reinhard. Antony Polonsky writes, "The total number of those murdered in three stages is now accepted to be around 6 million."[54] This figure includes all Jews murdered, not only those in Poland.

According to recent research, in the years 1939–45, between 5.6 million and 5.8 million Polish citizens were killed, of whom about 3 million were Jewish and 2.6 million to 2.8 million were mostly ethnically Polish, but also Ukrainian, Belarusian, and other minorities with Polish citizenship.[55]

Some Poles died in labor camps such as Auschwitz-Birkenau, Dachau, Stutthof, and Treblinka. Some were killed at the front, and others by the Soviets, including military officers and intellectuals in Katyń, where Polish Jews were also victims. The Catholic Church was severely attacked because the Church supported aspirations for freedom and maintaining the Polish national identity.[56]

It is difficult to determine how many Jews were

saved and how many people provided help. There are many theories about this. The Jewish historian Polonsky wrote:

> The records of the Central Committee of Jews in Poland (CKŻP), the main Jewish body in postwar Poland, reveal that 20,000 Jews survived on the "Aryan" side.[57] This figure is certainly too low, because many Jews kept their new identity or, for other reasons, did not register with the CKŻP. It should probably be doubled or even tripled. This would yield a figure of 40,000–60,000 Jews who survived as a result of Polish assistance (between 1.2% and 1.8% of the estimated 1939 Jewish population of 3,300,000). Not all hidden Jews survived the war, either because of denunciations or because they were discovered in random searches. Teresa Prekerowa estimated that only half of those who moved to the "Aryan side" lived long enough to see liberation. She also tried to estimate how many Poles were involved in the rescue of the Jews. According to this calculation, since it took more than one Pole to rescue a Jew, to reach a figure of how many Poles were involved in

rescuing Jews one would have to multiply the number of survivors by two or three. This gives a figure of between 160,000 and 360,000 Poles who, at the risk of their own lives and those of their families, helped save Jews.[58]

Polonsky offers the following comments on these numbers:

How do you evaluate these figures? Only one who was willing to risk his life in this way is able to do it. One such person is Władysław Bartoszewski, who wrote: "The moral question remains. From a moral perspective, it must be clearly stated that neither in Poland nor elsewhere in occupied Europe was enough done. 'Enough' was done only by those who died."[59]

In response to these words, Polonsky points to a statement of Yisrael Gutman, a leading Holocaust historian, who participated in the Warsaw ghetto uprising and survived imprisonment in Auschwitz:

Sometimes I hear Jews accusing the Poles of deliberately not helping them, even though they

72 *Chapter 3*

Fragebogen zur erstmaligen Meldung der Heilberufe.

Kwestionariusz dla pierwszego zgłoszenia zawodów leczniczych.

Heilberufe im Sinne dieser Meldung sind: Ärzte, Apotheker, Zahnärzte, Dentisten mit Berechtigung selbständige Praxis auszuüben, Zahntechniker ohne Berechtigung selbständige Praxis auszuüben, Feldschere, Hebammen, Krankenpfleger, Krankenpflegerinnen, Krankenschwestern, Masseure und Masseusen, Sprechstundenhilfen, Laborantinnen, Desinfektoren.

Die Fragebogen müssen gewissenhaft und sorgfältig ausgefüllt und deutlich geschrieben werden. Vor der Ausfüllung sind zunächst sämtliche Fragen zu lesen.

Gesundheitskammer des Distrikts: Kraków
Kreishauptmannschaft: Jarosław
Kreis: Jarosław
Art des Heilberufes: Technik dentystyczny

1. Familienname (bei Frauen auch Geburtsname): Goldmann
2. Vornamen (Rufnamen unterstreichen): Mechel
3. Ständiger Wohnort und Wohnung: Łańcut, ul. Mościckiego 21
4. Praxisstelle bezw. Arbeitsstätte: Łańcut
   a) bei selbständigen Heilberufen Praxisstelle:
   b) bei angestellten Heilberufen Arbeitsstätte (Arbeitgeber, Krankenhaus, Klinik usw.): Antoni Bielatowicz, Łańcut
5. Heimatanschrift: Łańcut
6. Tag, Monat und Jahr der Geburt: 15 września 1914
   Geburtsort: Łańcut   Kreis: Łańcut
7. Sind Sie ledig, verh., verwitwet, geschieden? wolny
   Der Ehefrau a) Mädchenname: /   b) Geburtsdatum: /
8. Zahl und Geburtsjahr der Kinder (die Verstorbenen in Klammern):
   1. /   2. /   3. /
9. Religiöses Bekenntnis: mojżeszowe
10. Staatsangehörigkeit am 1. 9. 1939: Polska

Zahntechniker Laborant

Questionnaire completed by Mechel Goldman as part of the application of medical professionals in the General Government (see also next page). The data provided established family connections and relationships with Markowa. Source: AŻIH

The War 73

11. a) des Angefragten:	Name	Vorname	Konf.	Volkstum
	Goldmann	Mechel	mojżesiowe	Polska
Vatersvater:	Goldmann	Chana	mojżesiowe	Polska
Vatersmutter:	Sauer	Abe	mojżesiowe	Polska
Muttervater:	Sauer	Hena	mojżesiowe	Polska
Muttermutter:				
b) seiner Ehefrau:	Name	Vorname	Konf.	Volkstum
	/	/	/	/
Vatersvater:	/	/	/	/
Vatersmutter:	/	/	/	/
Muttervater:	/	/	/	/
Muttermutter:	/	/	/	/

12. Wann (Tag, Monat, Jahr) und wo haben Sie Ihre Prüfung abgelegt?

13. Genaues Datum der Berechtigungserteilung: 4 marca 1933

14. Ort der Berechtigungserteilung: Lwów

15. Falls Berechtigung im Ausland erworben: Haben Sie die Genehmigung zur Ausübung Ihres Heilberufes innerhalb Polens?

Datum: und Aktenzeichen des Ministeriums:

16. Wann und an welcher Ausbildungsanstalt haben Sie Ihren Heilberuf erlernt? Zakład Lecz. Dentys. upraw. + deutytystyce + Bielatowice

17. Sind Sie früher im Dienst des Staates, der Länder und Gemeinden, der Wehrmacht oder in Ihren Berufsorganisationen hauptamtlich tätig gewesen? /

In welcher Eigenschaft? /

18. Haben Sie eine besondere Prüfung abgelegt? /

19. Üben Sie Ihren Heilberuf aus?

20. Ist Ihnen die Ausübung Ihres Heilberufes verboten? nie

21. Haben Sie auf die Ausübung Ihres Heilberufes verzichtet? nie

(Ein Verzicht ist der Gesundheitskammer Krakau schriftlich anzuzeigen).

22. Haben Sie am Weltkriege 1914—1918 teilgenommen? nie

In der Wehrmacht welchen Staates? / Damaliger Dienstgrad?

23. a) Haben Sie der polnischen Wehrmacht angehört? tak, jako sanitarjusz

could have. Such remarks are expressions of sorrow, eclipsing a sensitive attitude. More could have been done to save the Jews, but the Poles, under the conditions of occupation, could not have radically changed the fate of the Jews. The Allies perhaps could have done so, but even that is certainly not in the final stages of the madness of the murderers. Let me say more: there is no moral imperative that requires an ordinary mortal to risk his life and that of his family to save his fellow man. Are we capable of imagining the agony of fear of an individual, of a family who selflessly and voluntarily, only out of an inner human impulse, brings someone threatened with death into their home? Are we able to comprehend the pressure of those fears when a fugitive had to be kept out of sight of neighbors and relatives, when a neighbor or friend dared not hear the cough of a sick person nearby, and those hiding the fugitive lived in endless fear, when what was enough was a search of the house for both the hider and the hiding person that could end their lives? Poles should be proud that we have so many beacons of righteousness, which Ringelblum mentioned, who

> are the true heroes of the flood. And we can
> never do enough to thank these rare people.[60]

Bishops, nuns, and priests were very active in helping the Jewish population. According to the latest research, more than 2,500 nuns and religious from about 100 religious orders in more than 500 religious houses helped Jewish people. In addition, more than 700 diocesan priests in 600 locations across the country offered their help during the tumultuous years of the Holocaust.[61] And this was the most difficult time in terms of the persecution of the Church in Poland, because the Nazis sent to concentration camps, evicted, or prevented the pastoral ministry of about 50 percent of diocesan priests, and killed 20 percent of them.

While there were many who helped the Jews, there were also those who handed them over to the Germans, looted their goods, and even murdered them. Again, Antony Polonsky described the situation:

> In Poland, like everywhere in Europe, the response of those who witnessed the demarcation, ghettoization, deportation, and murder of their neighbors was complex. There were those who helped the Nazis by pointing out Jews or taking

possession of their property. Most people were terrified of the brutal Nazi rule and were only interested in surviving, showing indifference to the fate of others. But there were also those who for moral or religious reasons risked their lives to help those who faced death at Nazi hands.[62]

In addition to individual aid, there was some help from the Polish state. In September 1942, the Temporary Committee for Aid to the Jews, named after Konrad Żegota, was established. On December 4, it was transformed into the Żegota Council for Aid to Jews at the Delegation of the Government of the Republic of Poland. The council provided Jews with false documents, helped them find hiding places, and provided material support and medical care.[63]

Diplomatic assistance from Polish institutions abroad was also important and was exemplified by the Aleksander Ładoś group in Switzerland, which was one of the groups that provided passports, particularly to Latin American countries.[64] Thousands of Jews were saved this way.[65]

People from a certain locality who were saved from the Holocaust often started communities, especially in Israel, North America, and South America. To describe the life of these communities before the Holocaust and to preserve the memory of those who died, "Memorial Books" (Yizkor Books) were created.[66] Holocaust survivors described over four hundred shtetls where Jews lived before the war. Accounts of World War II and the postwar period are often contained therein.[67]

In 1953, the State of Israel established the highest honor for those who selflessly saved Jewish people: the Medal of the Righteous Among the Nations. It is awarded by the Yad Vashem Martyrs and Heroes Memorial Institute in Jerusalem. To date, more than 29,000 people have been honored with this award. The largest group — more than 7,000 — comes from Poland.[68] The Yad Vashem Institute stresses that this number is not representative of the effort or the percentage of Jews saved per country, and notes, "The Righteous Numbers are not necessarily an indication of the actual number of those who have rendered aid in each country but reflect the cases that have been made available to Yad Vashem."[69]

In this context, it should be emphasized that in the territory of occupied Poland, hiding Jews was not only punishable by death, but the death penalty was actually imposed. The Ulma family is one example.

The Nazis often ordered that murdered Jews be buried in a single grave with the Polish families who tried to help them. This common and tragic fate testifies — better than many words — to these acts of friendship sealed in blood. Hiding Jews was, in many cases, a charity lived to the end, and memorialized in the grave.

Markowa

Markowa, located in the southeast of Poland,[70] is a village with a population of just over 4,000. It is within an hour's drive of the Ukrainian border. Historically, and to some extent still today, Markowa's economy has centered on agriculture.

Markowa lies within the territory of the Catholic Archdiocese of Przemyśl, a city approximately 300 kilometers south of Warsaw and 200 kilometers east of Kraków.

The village of Markowa was founded in the second half of the 1400s.[71] German settlers, among others, were brought to this region to cultivate the land. However, Polish language and culture became the dominant force in the following centuries. According to some sources, the surname *Ulma* could be a legacy of this past and might be linked to the town of Ulm in the Baden-Württemberg region of Germany.

Markowa was a rural village, relatively prosperous. It served as a laboratory for the practice of rights. The farmers owned the land, and the first cooperatives in Poland began there.

During the Ulma family's time, Markowa was already home to more than nine hundred dwellings and approximately four thousand residents.

In the neighboring village of Gać, the People's University was established. It drew in intellectuals and positively affected the social and political climate of the entire region.

The Peasants' Party played a key role in the 1930s by organizing strikes to demand better recognition of workers' rights. The first health insurance company started then, to safeguard people's health.

Markowa was also at the forefront of women's issues. Inspired by the local cooperative movement, a national women's magazine, *Kobieta Wiejska* (*Country Woman*), a groundbreaking initiative, was founded in 1939. Four issues were published before the winds of war swept away this project, which was important for enhancing women's roles.

There was a sizable Jewish community within Markowa's economically, socially, and politically vibrant culture. According to the 1921 census, there were 126 Jews in Markowa, a number that, aside from a few departures for family reasons, remained more or less constant until the outbreak of World War II. There were about thirty Jewish families. There were three *bet midrash*, Jewish houses of prayer, in the village. For more solemn services, the community went to the synagogue in nearby Łańcut. There was also a Jewish cemetery just outside of Markowa.

Markowa did not have a distinct Jewish quarter, unlike other areas in Poland. Instead, the Jewish community was dispersed throughout various parts of the village. However, a section of the village shared the same name, Kazimierz, as the Jewish quarter in Kraków.[72] At the time of the Ulmas, there were seven homes occupied by Jewish families in this section. Although Markowa is listed as one of the localities where Jewish people resided, it was one of the smallest.[73]

With the outbreak of World War II, Markowa became a perilous city for Jewish people and for the non-Jewish Poles who helped them. Józef and Wiktoria Ulma were aware of this; they saw it every day on the streets of their village. But that did not prevent them from opening their door to help their Jewish neighbors.

In late July and early August 1942, Operation Reinhard was implemented in and around Łańcut, the town closest to the village of Markowa. The operation, the purpose of which was the killing of all Jews in the

General Governorate of occupied Poland, had begun in March of the same year. The Germans enforced a residence ban on Jews in the Markowa region, too. This was the starting point of their deportation to the Pełkinie labor camp and then to the Bełżec extermination camp.

Some of the Jews of Markowa came to the Ulmas for help. A relationship had been established between them for years, with working, friendly, and neighborly encounters. And the Ulmas's great faith prompted them to welcome everyone without calculating the risk to themselves.

At first, Józef assisted his friends in the Jewish community in constructing shelters on the outskirts of the village and in the forest. Detailed reports show how he helped the Ryfkis, a family of four, to build a shelter in a ravine by a creek. Such shelters could not, however, be a permanent solution because the German Feldgendarmerie and the local police were constantly checking and searching both the village and its surroundings.

On December 13, 1942, the Germans ordered the mayor of Markowa to organize a roundup. Before noon, the mayor managed to inform the villagers of the action planned by the Nazi SS, thus allowing the people in hiding to better protect themselves in their shelters. But not all of them could save themselves. German gendarmes

82 Chapter 3

Two Jewish women from Markowa wearing armbands with the Star of David. Their shelter in ravines (which Józef Ulma helped to build) was found during the search ordered by the village head on the orders of the Germans. On December 14, 1942, they were shot by the German gendarmerie.

arrested twenty-five of the approximately fifty-four Jews hiding in these makeshift shelters. The prisoners were locked in the communal detention center at the village's main crossroads. On December 14, 1942, the German gendarmes of Łańcut shot every one. All died.

Poles living in Markowa during the German occupation also lived in fear of death: "For offenses deemed to be violations of German rigor, gendarmes from the Łańcut and Przeworsk posts at different times and under different circumstances killed fifty-nine inhabitants of Markowa."[74]

Despite these actions, twenty-nine Jews continued to hide in Markowa after December 1942, including the eight who hid in the Ulmas's house. Twenty-one survived to see the end of the occupation.

Chapter 4
THE MASSACRE

Why did Józef and Wiktoria decide to take such a great risk, hosting a group of Jews, when such action was utterly forbidden, under penalty of death, in Poland's occupied territories? Why did they risk their lives and those of their children?

The answer is as simple as it is profound: The decision flowed from their Christian Faith.

The testimonies and material gathered during the beatification cause indicate that the Ulmas decided to welcome these Jewish families with full awareness, knowing exactly the risks they faced. "They are people, and I will not throw them out," Józef replied to those who pointed out the danger they were putting themselves in.

Other witnesses, commenting on this decision, stressed how the Ulmas decided to be "practicing Catholics" — that is, to translate the Gospel and the parable of the Good Samaritan, underlined by them with a red pencil, into the concrete choices of their lives, no matter what it entailed. Some excerpts from other testimonies collected during the beatification process explain this difficult choice of the couple, driven by their total adherence to the Gospel:

- "I am convinced that the reception of these Jewish people, with all the consequences, was undertaken consciously and thoughtfully."
- "The heroic love of the Servants of God for their neighbors brought about their persecution."
- "Servants of God Józef and Wiktoria were raised in religious families, rooted in and practicing the Christian faith."
- "I knew Wiktoria's family, especially her mother: my mother's sister. She was a very religious person. And that is how she raised her children. I also knew Józef Ulma's parents; they were hardworking and devout. Józef and Wiktoria received a good family upbringing."[75]

They knew very well that they could be killed for hiding Jews. The windows of their house overlooked the trench where the Nazi brought Jews to be shot.[76] They saw people killed, yet they decided to save those they could. Even Antoni, Józef's brother, said to him, "Don't hide the Jews, because the consequences will be unhappy."[77]

All these testimonies lead inexorably to the conclusion that Józef's and Wiktoria's choice was related to their love for Christ and their will to put the Gospel into practice. That is also how they educated their children, who shared martyrdom with their parents.

In the introduction to his book, which recounts the story of the Ulma family, Polish Chief Rabbi Michael Schudrich asks, "How to write about the Righteous Among the Nations? Words fail. Words are inadequate to describe or convey the goodness that they exude. Simply put, the Righteous is an example of what God hoped for when God created human beings."[78]

March 24, 1944: The Slaughter

On the night of March 23–24, 1944, about ten military personnel — five German gendarmes and between four and six Blue Police (the local security forces supporting the Nazi occupiers) — arrived at the Ulma family home in Markowa. Lieutenant Eilert Dieken, the head of the Łańcut gendarmerie, commanded the group. To prevent anyone from escaping, they immediately surrounded the Ulma house, a farm building located about four hundred meters from the main road.

The tragic sequence of the events of that day was described in the trial of one of the gendarmes, Józef Kokott, 23, of Czech origin. An eyewitness, Edward Nawojski, reported in court that he drove the German gendarmes to the Ulmas's house and was forced to witness the massacre.

The murder of all those in the house was methodically conducted. No one was saved. Not even the children.

Three Jews were shot during their sleep in the attic of the house, and the others were shot shortly after in the back of their heads.

A photograph on the Ulmas' kitchen table, probably taken by Józef himself, now serves as indirect documentation of what happened that day. It depicts a happy moment in the village of Markowa, with a little girl and two older girls sitting on the ground, smiling at the camera; in the background is a man on a bicycle. That image, a symbol of peaceful daily life in Markowa before the war, was stained by a few drops of the blood of the murdered Jews that fell from the attic down to the floor below. Today, that photograph still bears the stains of the blood shed by these innocents.

The gendarmes forced Józef and Wiktoria, pregnant with their last child, out of their house. They killed the couple immediately, not allowing them to utter a word. The point-blank execution was intended to show the villagers what punishment would befall those who attempted to hide Jews.

A Chilling Order

After briefly consulting with his subordinates, Dieken also ordered the killing of the children. The little ones screamed, cried, and called for their parents, not knowing that they were already dead. But nothing stopped the killers' murderous rampage. Kokott killed three of the little ones. The other gendarmes murdered the remaining children.

Within a few minutes, seventeen people had been murdered, including the child Wiktoria held in her womb. At the moment of her execution, she began to give birth out of fear and shock. A witness present at the time of the exhumation of the bodies reported that he had seen the baby's head between his mother's legs.

Wiktoria's best friend, Stanislawa Kuźniar, who testified for the beatification process, recounted the moment she arrived at the Ulmas's home after the tragedy had just occurred:

> There were only traces of a gruesome crime. The bodies of the murdered had already been laid in the two graves dug in the house courtyard. It was a terrible sight. ... The house, which had always been teeming with life, was now empty; blood everywhere, in the attic, rooms, courtyard, blood, blood, blood. ... Unbearable. The whole house had been ransacked in search of precious objects which the executioners could not find, for there were none in this house. Everything was scattered. The photographs on the floor.[79]

Kokott, at the end of the massacre, uttered terrible words that remained forever imprinted in the mind of the witness, Edward Nawojski: "Look at how the Polish pigs that give shelter to the Jews die."[80] Nawojski reported this at the gendarme's trial. Among other Nazi executioners, in addition to Eilert Dieken, were Michael Dziewulski and Erich Wilde. In Markowa, they were known for their violent actions.

Looting and Revelry

After the massacre, the Germans looted the farm and the belongings of those they had murdered. They used a flashlight to find and steal everything of value. They searched the corpses down to the last pocket and took everything they could find. When they saw a small bag with jewelry on Gołda Grünfeld's chest, one of the gendarmes said, "This is what I needed," and put it in his pocket.[81]

The other Germans concentrated on the assets of the Ulmas: They took beds, mattresses, plates, and the leather that Józef had worked. Since the things they plundered did not fit in the carts they had brought with them, the Germans ordered the head of the village to bring two more.

Teofil Kielar, mayor of the village, was ordered to bury the victims with the help of other inhabitants who had witnessed what had happened. Kielar, at one point, armed himself with courage and asked the German commander, whom he knew from previous and frequent checkups and roundups, why the children had also been killed. Dieken was annoyed by the question and responded, "So that you and your village have no problems with them."

When one of the villagers called to bury those seventeen bodies battered by gunfire asked if they could bury the Jews and the Catholics separately, one of the gendarmes became irritated because they were wasting time and began to shoot again, sowing terror among the villagers. But then he consented to that request, and two pits were dug.

Finally, the perpetrators of the massacre drank at the scene of the execution to celebrate that horror accomplished without mercy. Kielar was forced to provide them with vodka, and, according to witnesses, they "drank at least three liters." Kokott finally told the witnesses not to report how many people had been killed, "Only you know this, and you must not tell anyone." He probably did not want to explain why the children had also been murdered.[82]

As for the youngest child, who was still in his mother's womb during her execution, the following testimonies are crucial. Teofil Kielar, the mayor of the village, who had been called by the Germans a few dozen minutes after the massacre to bury the bodies at the execution site, reported that, "As for Ulma Viktoria, she was indeed pregnant, from what was evident from her outward appearance."[83] However, he said nothing about her giving birth.

Four or five days after the tragic events, several people, including relatives of Józef and Wiktoria, went to the site of the massacre to exhume the family's bodies and place them in coffins and bury them again in the same place, in the hope that they could transfer them to the parish cemetery in the future. One of these men, Franciszek Szylar, testified: "Placing the body of Wiktoria Ulma in the coffin, I found that she was pregnant. I base my statement on the fact that from her reproductive organs, the head and chest of a baby were visible."[84]

Similarly, Roman Kluz, Wiktoria's nephew, recounts that when his father, Józef Niemczak, and Antoni Szpytma "brought the coffins to place the bodies in," "they found the seventh child born in the grave, which my aunt had given birth to after her death."[85]

Thus, based on these testimonies, we know that Wiktoria Ulma was buried in an advanced state of pregnancy, and that, after four or five days, when the villagers exhumed her body from the temporary burial, they noticed the baby's head and chest.

Several months after the massacre, on January 11, 1945, relatives of the Ulmas — once again defying Nazi restrictions — exhumed the bodies and moved them to the local parish cemetery. Two years later, the remains of the murdered Jews were unearthed and buried in Jagiełła Cemetery, along with the victims of the December 14, 1942, massacre.

Fate of the Perpetrators

The only gendarme prosecuted for the massacre in Markowa was Józef Kokott. In 1957, he was captured in Czechoslovakia, his country of origin, and brought to Poland for trial. After the proceedings held at the Rzeszów Regional Court in 1958, he was sentenced to death, but his sentence was later reduced to life imprisonment. After a change in the law, the penalty was decreased to 25 years imprisonment. He died in Bytom prison in 1980.

Włodzimierz Leś, the "blue policeman" and most likely the spy who reported the presence of Jews in the Ulma house, was tried and convicted by the Polish Underground State (Polskie Państwo Podziemne). On September 11, 1944, the Polish resistance sentenced him to death. According to documents kept by the Institute of National Remembrance, underground soldiers from the Polish resistance militias shot and killed him in Łańcut.

In contrast, after the war, Eilert Dieken, the commander of this horrible operation against the Ulma family and their Jewish guests, peacefully performed police work in Essen, Lower Saxony, Germany. By the time the prosecutor's office at the Dortmund Regional Court opened an investigation in the 1960s into crimes committed by the German gendarmerie in the occupied district of Jarosław, Dieken had already died. He had passed away in 1960 as an ordinary, respected citizen and not as the criminal he had been during Poland's occupation. Neither he nor any of the remaining perpetrators of the massacre at the Ulmas' home ever saw the inside of a courtroom.

Jews Hiding in Markowa after the Ulmas Were Killed

The news of the murder of the Ulma family and of the eight Jews they had hid spread quickly throughout the village. But this did not deter other families from continuing to help their Jewish friends and neighbors. According to accounts from the time, at least twenty Jews survived because they found hiding places in the homes of farmers in this Polish village.

Józef and Julia Bar and their daughter Janina showed great hospitality by providing a haven in their home for the Riesenbachs, a family of five, for nearly two years. So did Antoni and Dorota Szylar, who offered refuge in their barn to the Weltz family. At first, the Weltzes begged the farmer to let them hide for a few days. Later, realizing that they could not move from that place without risking their lives, they asked Antoni to let them stay longer. Thanks to the Szylar's hospitality, all seven mem-

Meal in the family home of Wiktoria Ulma. From left: Maria née Cwynar, her husband Józef Niemczak; on the right, three sons of the Niemczaks: Stanisław, Jan, and Antoni.

bers of the family were able to survive the war.

Stanisława Kuźniar, the Ulmas' friend, spoke of seeing abnormal movements in the Szylar house. There, too, as in Wiktoria's family, much more food was being prepared than the family needed. When she saw in their kitchen a pot full of *kluski śląskie*, the typical Polish dumplings, and asked who all that food was for, she would hear such answers as "It's for the cat, too," or "It's also for the dog."

One day, Stanisława noticed a group of people lined up behind the house, reaching out for a dish of food provided by Dorota Szylar. Stanisława Kuźniar observed this without asking any questions, remaining silent as she had previously done when she witnessed a man crafting leather behind the Ulma residence. Little did she know this man was one of their Jewish guests. Only later did she realize the extraordinary heroism of these Markowa families, who had decided to help and house Jews to save them from the Nazis.

Michał Bar, another Markowa resident in those difficult years, offered shelter to the three people of the Lorbenfeld family. Jan and Weronika Przybylak rescued Jakub Einhorn and a family of three.

Abraham Segal survived the war by hiding at Helena and Jan Cwynar's house and pretending to be a cattle rancher. At the end of the war, he moved to Haifa, Israel. Abraham had three children and a dozen grandchildren. He always maintained contact with the citizens of Markowa, thanks to whose generosity he managed to survive the fury of war and Nazi persecution. Out of gratitude, Segal sponsored many visits of young people from Israel, his new homeland, to the village of Markowa.

Abraham Segal died in Israel in 2019. In a message

sent for his funeral, Polish President Andrzej Duda, who had honored the deceased with the Cross of Merit of the Republic of Poland in 2016, emphasized:

> The truth about the ages of co-existence on Polish soil, about the tragic fate of our nations during the German occupation, about the Holocaust, and heroism of those who risked their lives to help their Jewish co-citizens and neighbors, is the foundation on which we should build our future. Abraham Segal was a promoter of this message to future generations.[86]

Jewish people also found refuge during the war in the area surrounding Markowa. As Stanisław Dobosz describes it:

> In Gać, eleven Jews found refuge with the families of Jan Solarz, Jan and Wojciech Kuźniar, and Michał Świątek; in Białoboki with Stanisław Szpiłyk; in Sietesz with Michał Dupczyński and Michał Płachta; and in Chodakówka per family two people of this nationality found refuge and protection.[87]
>
> Jewish people took refuge in forests and

groves, away from buildings. They, too, benefited from various forms of aid from the local population. In the Gać countryside, a family of four hid for a year in a pit dug in the ramparts of Ziębowa, in the so-called Great Pit. In Chodakówka, eleven Jews camped in the same conditions. Despite the attention, in July 1941, the gendarmes discovered the campers and shot them on the spot. … A total of 119 Jews died in the territory of the Markowa municipality.[88]

In total, more than twenty Jews were rescued in Markowa, and dozens more in the countryside near the village.

Chapter 5
RIGHTEOUS AND BLESSED

Józef and Wiktoria Ulma were awarded the title of "Righteous Among the Nations" in 1995. In 2010, Polish President Lech Kaczyński posthumously awarded them the Commander's Cross of the Order of Polonia Restituta, one of the country's most prestigious honors.

March 24, the day of the Ulma family's death, has been celebrated in Poland as the National Day of Remembrance for Poles Who Rescued Jews since 2018. This day honors all those who helped the Jewish population under German occupation despite great danger to themselves.

Yad Vashem in Jerusalem also recognized the Szylar and Bar families of Markowa as Righteous Among the Nations. The Jewish community has awarded several thousand Poles this sign of recognition. Poland is among the nations with the greatest number of people who have been honored as Righteous Among the Nations.

The Ulmas were recognized posthumously, but some Poles among the Righteous were honored during their lifetime. These individuals could provide firsthand accounts of their families' significant efforts to help their Jewish friends.

In November 2018, the Pontifical Urban University (the Urbaniana) and the Foundation of the Ulma Family SOAR organized a symposium and photo exhibition in Rome, entitled *Honoring the Righteous*, dedicated to the Ulma family. The event was attended by a group of Poles who have received the title Righteous Among the Nations from Israel.

Pope Francis and the Ulmas

Pope Francis participated in World Youth Day in July 2016, hosted in Kraków, in the home country of WYD founder Pope St. John Paul II.

The most touching moment of Pope Francis' apostolic journey came on July 29, when he visited the Auschwitz-Birkenau concentration camp. The pope did not utter a word, but that silence is still worth more today than many speeches or homilies.

The only words Pope Francis left that day were those he wrote in his native Spanish on the camp's book of remembrance: "*Señor ten piedad de tu pueblo! Señor, perdón por tanta crueldad!*" ("Lord, have mercy on your people! Lord, forgive for so much cruelty!").

Pope Francis then chose to pray in solitude on a bench next to the wall where prisoners were shot and spent fifteen minutes in the shadows of Cell 18, the so-called starvation bunker, where St. Maximilian Kolbe, the Franciscan who sacrificed his life for the sake of a man with a family, was imprisoned.

The Pontiff's pilgrimage to that place of sorrows began with the slow entry, head down, into the camp that still bears the inscription *Arbeit Macht Frei* (Work Makes Free), the sinister motto the Nazis had posted at the entrance to that factory of death. Then Pope Francis kissed one of the beams of the pole from which prisoners were hung and rested his head on the wall of the *Appellplatz*, where the daily roll calls of prisoners were held. Ten survivors who had lived through the horror of that concentration camp were with him on that silent visit, and the pope embraced them one by one.

On that July day, Pope Francis concluded his visit to Auschwitz by presiding at an interreligious ceremony in which the *kaddish* sung by the chief rabbi of Poland alternated with the reading of Psalm 130, the *De Profundis*. Fr. Stanisław Ruszała, the parish priest of Markowa, recited the psalm and later introduced the pope to the history of the Ulma family, the Polish Samaritans.

When greeting Polish pilgrims during his general audience on November 28, 2018, Pope Francis also addressed the organizers of the exhibition at the Pontifical Urban University that honored the Ulma family: "May this large Family of Servants of God, which awaits beatification, be an example for all of us of fidelity to God and to His commandments, of love of one's neighbor and respect for human dignity."[89]

Since the beginning of his papacy, Pope Francis has consistently acknowledged the immense tragedy of the Shoah. He has noted that, despite the extensive knowledge of the atrocities committed during World War II, certain forms of anti-Semitism continue to resurface. Pope Francis released a message on November 9, 2021, the anniversary of Kristallnacht, which reads in part: "Let us commit ourselves to promoting education for brotherhood, so that the regurgitations of hatred that would like to destroy do not prevail. The menace of anti-Semitism, which is still snaking through Europe and elsewhere, is a fuse that must be put out."[90]

Many survivors of the Holocaust have met Pope Francis in public or private audiences. Some of the most poignant images from such meetings occur when the pope gently touches the tattoo of someone's concentration camp identification. When he met the Polish writer Lidia Maksymowicz in 2021, she uncovered her arm to show him her mark as a former Nazi death camp prisoner. Pope Francis looked at her for a few moments, then leaned down and kissed her on that very number, 70072, which, after more than seventy years, remains a daily reminder of the horror she experienced.

Path to Beatification

The beatification process of the Ulma family began in 2003. At first, Józef, Wiktoria, and their children were part of a larger group of World War II martyrs. But in 2017, at the request of Archbishop Adam Szal of Przemyśl, the Congregation (now Dicastery) for the Causes of Saints decided to separate their cause for beatification from the group of martyrs, citing the uniqueness of their story — namely, that an entire family had been killed: both parents, six children, and one unborn child. Five years later, on December 17, 2022, Pope Francis issued the decree acknowledging the martyrdom of the Venerable Servants of God, initiating their beatification.

According to Archbishop Stanisław Gądecki, Metropolitan of Poznań and President of the Polish Bishops' Conference, "the Ulma family has become an example of love." Archbishop Gądecki emphasizes "the beauty of the souls of the righteous, the purity of this precious pearl" that "shines before our eyes, leaving an example to follow. A model that teaches us to trust God's promises."[91]

Archbishop Szal notes that the beatification of the Ulma family is an unprecedented event:

> With an act of beatification, the entire family is elevated to the glory of the altars: the parents Józef and Wiktoria Ulma with their seven children. A further unprecedented fact is that the beatification also extends to the unborn child in the womb at the time of martyrdom. They were martyred because they dared to welcome eight people of Jewish origin under their roof in hardships of war, having previously helped other Jews persecuted only because they were of that origin and not another.

Father Burda, the postulator of the beatification process, who examined all the documentation on the case, declares that love of neighbor was the crucial element of the Ulma family's life:

> The Ulma family embraced the Gospel very maturely, especially the call to Christian love of one's neighbor. In the Bible, found in their home after the execution, the title of the parable of the Good Samaritan is underlined. It shows their daily life centered on the Gospel and union with God, following the call to obedience. It also teaches the value of every human as created in God's image and likeness.

Bishop Stanisław Jamrozek, the auxiliary bishop of the Archdiocese of Przemyśl and the first postulator for the beatification process at the diocesan level, focuses on the core values of the Ulma family's Christian beliefs and the beatification of their unborn child:

> The couple's deep love for God and people and their willingness to make sacrifices is most evident in their love for children. They always welcomed new life with great openness.
>
> Then, there was a great and courageous love toward the Jews they were hiding at the time. Their life is an excellent testimony to the world: Love, even in the most challenging circumstances, still shows its face, and this is a re-

sponse to the love of the Lord God himself. ...

When one loves God, one can also love the persons God places in one's life's journey. Above all, this beatification of an unborn child is a recognition that a baby in the mother's womb is a human being and that that person deserves protection and care.[92]

Martyrdom

There are two ways a beatification process can proceed. The Church may decide that a person is blessed or, later, a saint after their "heroicity of the Christian virtues" has been verified through testimonies and documents and, subsequently, a miracle — a scientifically inexplicable healing — can be attributed to his or her intercession. The other way is the attestation of martyrdom or Christian acceptance of one's death imposed out of hatred of the Faith. The latter path is no longer exclusively applied, as it had been for centuries, to those who choose to accept death rather than to renounce their faith but is also applied to those who accept death because of their faithful adherence to Christ to the end.

Although there are testimonies of miracles attributed to intercession by the Ulma family, the path chosen for their beatification has been martyrdom, because there is sufficient evidence of the material of martyrdom in the circumstances of the family's murder by Nazi policemen on March 24, 1944, along with the Jews they were hiding.

In a formal determination of martyrdom, the Church must consider "*ex parte persecutoris,*" or the persecutor's part — that is, the purpose intended by those who bring about the death of the victims. In this case, the man who commanded the murders was Eilert Diecken, and one of the perpetrators was gendarme Joseph Kokott. "These two persons," according to the Dicastery for the Causes of Saints,

> were moved by anti-Semitic hatred and a prevailing anti-Christian aversion that is not remote or merely theoretical. Even though gendarmerie regulations did not require it, Diecken reneged from the Christian, evangelical faith when he joined the Nazi police. Even Kokott, though not a member of the SS, wore on his cap the "dead head" that distinguished members of Satanist and esoteric Himmlerian groups, the very groups to which Diecken probably belonged.[93]

Diecken personally selected those who made up the firing squad that executed the Ulmas, making sure that the fiercest gendarmes, including Kokott, handled the deed. Those gendarmes were on duty in the village and were aware of the Catholic dedication of the Ulmas as well as their Gospel-based hospitality, free from the desire for financial gain.

Then there is the killing of the children: Infanticide could find no justification in any penal procedure. Kokott personally killed three or four of the Ulma children. The executioners reacted violently to the request for separate burials for Jews and Christians, threatening the gravedigger by firing several shots, even though the request was eventually granted. And finally, the massacre was celebrated, as in a macabre ritual, with sneers and vodka.

According to the Dicastery for the Causes of Saints, all of these elements indicate that the purpose of the persecutors was kill this family for their adherence to the Faith.

Theologians from the Dicastery for the Causes of Saints have determined that these murders were carried out not so much because the Ulmas were Catholics but because, in their daily lives, they were true Christians and observed Christ's command to love their neighbor. That command was for them above all other laws, including the laws imposed by the Nazis. The heinous murder of the entire family found its cause in this.

Regarding the conditions of formal martyrdom *ex parte victimarum*, or on the part of the victims, the Dicastery for the Causes of the Saints notes that the Ulmas attended their parish; they went to Mass every Sunday and on holy days; on Sundays, they did not work and always celebrated the Lord's Day with friends and relatives. They also welcomed with joy, despite the economic hardship of doing so, all of the children with whom they had been blessed over a short span of years.

Since childhood, Józef and Wiktoria were both members of the Living Rosary Confraternity, committing themselves to pray daily.

The day of their martyrdom, March 24, 1944, in the church of Saint Dorothy in Markowa, confessions had been held to prepare for Easter. Again, according to several testimonies collected by the Dicastery of the Causes of Saints, Józef and Wiktoria likely participated in this celebration, considering their active involvement in the life of the parish. And just as the martyrdom of Fr. Maximilian Kolbe occurred on August 14, 1941, on the eve of the feast of the Assumption of Our Lady, March 24 is the eve of the feast of the Annunciation of the Blessed

Virgin Mary. For some years now, March 25 has been Sanctity of Life Day in Poland and in many other countries around the world. It is a symbolic date in light of the Catholic Church recognizing, for the first time in history, an unborn child as a martyr.

The Ulmas's "choice to help the Jews was considered in the light of the commandment of love and the example of the Good Samaritan, as shown by the underscores written on their Bible," the Dicastery for the Causes of Saints notes. "The children were baptized and involved in the active faith of their parents. For the unborn child, there was the Baptism of blood."

Regarding the Ulmas' unborn child, "The Church is full of theological arguments," explains Father Burda, the postulator for the Ulmas's cause, "which helped us to show to the theologians of the Dicastery of the Causes of Saints that even that child without a name or Baptism can be considered a martyr for the faith of Christ." The Polish priest, who has led the cause of beatification of the Ulmas in recent years, recalls in this regard the martyrdom of the Holy Innocents, the children who were killed in Bethlehem at the behest of King Herod. A similar martyrdom "continues to this day, with so many children, especially the unborn, discarded by humans,"[94] Father Burda adds.

In addition to the recognition of the martyrdom of the baby who was just about to be born as a result of his mother's severe shock and fear during the execution, the six remaining siblings are also among the youngest martyrs ever recognized in the Catholic Church. The oldest, Stasia, was seven years old at the time of her death; the youngest, Marysia, had turned one year old just a few months before her murder.

The reputation of the martyred Ulma family has remained high over time, despite the complex historical events that unfolded in Poland throughout the twentieth century. Their story has come down to the present day, coupled with a certain *fama signorum* or popular belief in the efficacy of their intercession before God. While the Ulmas are blessed because they are martyrs, and this was the process the Church followed for their beatification, miracles are believed to have occurred through their intercession.

Fr. Witold Burda, the postulator for the Ulmas's cause, has for several years been part of a movement called "Luce e Vita" (founded in 1954 by Fr. Franciszek Blachnicki), in which he is mainly involved in family ministry. He has seen for himself the effects of the Ulmas's intercession:

Working with many couples as spiritual father and confessor and organizing many family retreats, I can testify to this. I entrust each of these meetings to the Ulma family.

I could recount hours and hours of the beautiful testimonies of couples and families who participated.

I can also tell about several couples who, after getting married, could not have children and turned to the diocesan Caritas of Przemyśl for help from a medical point of view.

The people at the Caritas Center always invite them to pray to the Ulma family. We have at least three cases of whom we are all convinced that the wives became pregnant thanks to the intercession of this martyred Polish family. Today, they are happy families.[95]

A Story from Maryland

The intercession of the Ulma family has been felt beyond the borders of Poland, as a story from the U.S. state of Maryland, reported in March 2023 by the Catholic news service OSV News, shows.[96]

Kelly Lindquist was three months pregnant with her seventh child when her husband, Ian, was diagnosed with leukemia. It was March 24, 2021. That same day, Kelly learned of another family with six children and a seventh on the way who lived in Poland in the early 20th century: Servants of God Józef and Wiktoria Ulma. They had been killed by the Nazis 77 years earlier, to the day — March 24, 1944 — along with the Jews they had taken into their home, who belonged to the Goldman, Grünfeld, and Didner families.

"Ian was diagnosed with leukemia on the feast of the Ulma family or their death day. I was pregnant with our seventh child at the time, just like Wiktoria was pregnant with her seventh child when they were killed," Kelly Lindquist recalled. "Our Catholic doctor said, 'You need to pray to this family for a miracle.'"

From that moment on, a new chapter opened in the family's daily prayer life, but they also went through a process of drawing closer to God and to each other. "From the moment he was diagnosed with this disease, we spent about a year and a month together, and the Ulma family was with us all along," Lindquist said.

A friend of the family requested that some relics of the Ulma family be shipped from Poland to the Lindquist family in Maryland. The people of Markowa did not hesitate to deliver some items to these people whom they did not know but who had asked them for help.

They sent a book with Józef's signature, a small rosary made from the wood of the Ulma family's garden tree, and a piece of wood from Wiktoria's family home. The Lindquists received with joy these objects, which they respected as precious relics.

"I remember one day, pregnant with my baby, I was in bed next to my husband, who did not look good. I really felt like he could die that night. It was getting worse, and I felt the Ulmas there with me," Kelly said. "I was praying and felt as if the Ulmas were truly caring for me, the child, our children, and Ian."

"Over time, my children received so many graces, and I attribute them to the children of Ulma. We pray to them every evening, remembering them all by their name. They have accompanied us, and we have felt their presence very strong all the time," Kelly added.

Ian Lindquist, an education scholar at the Ethics and Public Policy Center in Washington, D.C., died of leukemia on May 5, 2022.

When asked if she felt disappointed that the miracle she had hoped for had not transpired, Kelly Lindquist responded, "I never felt like the miracle didn't happen. I realized that the miracles that God had given us through the intercession of the Ulma family had been huge. Miracles of knots tied in our marriage, all being unknotted and washed away."

"God made a great miracle for us. The Ulma family brought us a great miracle. The small miracle," she said, referring to the hoped-for healing of her husband, "never arrived. Although Ian remained alive much longer than he should or we would have expected, considering his illness."

The real miracle, the greatest they could have received, and which they did receive through prayers to the Polish family, was "to be together, to love one another here on this earth."

One month after Ian's death, Kelly felt she needed to thank the people of Markowa for the items they had sent, and especially for the entire village's months of prayers for Ian's recovery.

"I felt very strongly I wanted to go and say thank you to them," she said. "I wanted to see where the Ulma family had died. I wanted to see where they lived. I wanted to meet their family and say thank you to their village just for all the graces that they had given to us in that time that we had with my husband."

So, with a friend's help, she packed her seven young children onto a flight to Europe and arrived in Markowa, Poland, in the summer of 2022. Kelly Lindquist and her children visited the Museum of Poles

Who Saved Jews in World War II, where Ulma family memorabilia is displayed.

In Poland, they were guests of Wiktoria Ulma's relatives, who organized a big party for the American family. Kelly gave the rosary she had received from Poland to Urszula Niemczak, the wife of Wiktoria's nephew, who hosted them on their visit to Markowa. "This rosary was, for me, the first sign of the Ulma family beatification," Niemczak said. "The rosary that Kelly gave us we pray every night. It is like a relic to us, a sign of victory of life over death. It is the biggest weapon for the lack of love in people's hearts."

For Kelly Lindquist, the Ulma family is an example to follow and to give thanks for. "It was a grace that Ian got to see our child and that we all got to be together as a family for about a year because the baby was nine months old when Ian died."

CONCLUSION

The story of the Ulma family is unprecedented. "The importance and novelty of this beatification [of the Ulma family] rest in the fact that it unites Józef and Wiktoria with all their young children who were killed with them, including the one still in the womb," wrote the Consultor for the Dicastery for the Causes of Saints, Fr. François-Marie Léthel, in the papal newspaper *L'Osservatore Romano*.[97]

Father Léthel continues:

> The beatification of the seventh child still in the womb is surely the most unique and important element. This nameless child, whose sex is not even known, was born neither naturally nor supernaturally in baptism but only in the life of Heaven. To the Church, he (or she) is a person and a holy person; a soul who sees the face of God and represents in the Church of Heaven the immense crowd of children who died before birth by natural death or death caused by abortion. Speaking of this beatification, it is worth

mentioning how, after the Council, the Church overcame the classic doctrine of limbo, which forever excluded all infants who died without baptism from the life of Heaven. In 2007, Pope Benedict XVI approved the document of the International Theological Commission, which, while reaffirming the importance of baptism, opens the firm hope of eternal salvation for these infants. Here, great Gospel insight is given to us in the Visitation narrative, when Jesus, already present and alive in Mary's womb, sanctifies John the Baptist in Elizabeth's womb. In the words of St. Irenaeus of Lyon, the Incarnation of the Son of God is truly "the recapitulation of the long history of mankind," of everyone in particular, from the moment of his or her conception. Before birth and before baptism, Jesus unites with every human being as his Creator and Savior. "Where sin increased, grace overflowed all the more" (Romans 5:20).[98.]

We wanted to tell the Ulmas's story not only because this family evokes such emotion — just look at the ruffled, smiling children — but because their heroism and martyrdom can serve as an example and ultimately give people hope. Józef and Wiktoria, with their children Stasia, Basia, Władziu, Franio, Antoś, Marysia, and the unnamed baby, have shown that love — the true kind — does not calculate. Love does not spare the one who loves from discomfort and risk. Love goes all the way, even to the point of "laying down one's life for one's friends," in the words of the Gospel of John.

Saul Goldman and his sons — Baruch, Mechel, Joachim, and Moses — were killed with the Ulmas, as were the two sisters (daughters of Chaim Goldman, a relative of Saul) Gołda Grünfeld and Lea (Layka) Didner, and Lea's young daughter, Reszla. "We could call it a 'Jewish-Christian martyrdom,'" wrote the Consultor for the Dicastery for the Causes of Saints.[99]

During the terrible years of the Second World War, there were many stories of heroism like that of the Ulmas. One of the best known must certainly be the story of St. Maximilian Kolbe. A Franciscan priest, Kolbe was sent to the Auschwitz concentration camp in 1941. He offered to replace a husband and father who was to be locked in the so-called starvation bunker. Kolbe survived this torture but was executed by the injection of carbolic acid. Franciszek Gajowniczek (the family man saved by Kolbe's generous gesture) survived and was in St. Peter's Square on October 10, 1982, when Pope John

Paul II proclaimed the Polish Franciscan friar a saint.

"No one has greater love than this, to lay down one's life for one's friends." Pope John Paul II opened his homily at the canonization of St. Maximilian Kolbe with this verse from the Gospel of John (15:13). Many other Polish bishops, priests, women religious, and nuns paid with their lives during World War II for standing by people, standing in solidarity with persecuted Jews, and standing firm in the values of the Christian Faith.

On June 13, 1999, in Warsaw during his seventh visit to Poland, Pope John Paul II beatified 108 Polish martyrs who were victims during the Nazi occupation Poland from 1939 to 1945. The large group of martyrs consisted of bishops, diocesan priests, men and women religious, and laypeople. They all suffered torture and mistreatment, were imprisoned, and many spent their final moments in the infamous concentration camps of Dachau, Auschwitz, Treblinka, Sutthof, Ravensbrück, or Sachsenhausen; they were subjected to the gas chamber, beheading, shooting, hanging, or were beaten to death by camp guards. In most cases, their bodies were never recovered.

Some managed to survive while risking everything to stand in solidarity with Jews and, above all, to remain faithful to the Christian love described in the Gospel.

Among these individuals are those Israel has honored with the title "Righteous Among the Nations." In November 2018, during the event organized by the Pontifical Urban University with the Ulma Family Foundation SOAR, some of these "Righteous" attended the event to discuss the family from Markowa. In Toruń, Poland, is the "Chapel of Remembrance," which bears more than 1,200 names of Poles killed for helping Jews.[100] Toruń is also home to Memorial Park, which includes more than 30,000 names of Poles who helped Jews during the Holocaust.

In contrast to these heroic stories of Poles unhesitatingly risking their lives to help Jews, there were people in Poland who adapted to the inhumane situation during the war and occupation and collaborated with the Nazis. Poland has also suffered anti-Semitic behavior before the Holocaust, during the Holocaust, and after World War II.

The purpose of this book is to present the history of the Ulma family and the Goldman, Didner, and Grünfeld families, leaving the discussion of anti-Semitism to historians who are involved in the study of the Holocaust. Through this book, we want to preserve the memory of these Jewish families, innocent victims of the Holocaust, and the Polish family who gave their lives to save them. Their courage, love, and hope for a better future remain a beacon that lights our way.

AFTERWORD (THE GENESIS OF A BOOK)

There are some stories you stumble upon by accident that then somehow change your life. In December 2022, I was at the Rzeszów airport in Poland, near the Ukrainian border. Until February 24, 2022, Rzeszów had been a peripheral airstrip in the Polish transportation system. On that day, however, it suddenly found itself at the center of history: a crossroads of arrivals and departures, a hub for humanitarian (and also military) aid in the wake of Russia's invasion of Ukraine.

On the second floor of the airport — where, through the large glass walls you can see, on the same runway, the planes of discount airlines taking families on vacation to warm, exotic places and NATO anti-aircraft missile batteries — there is a chapel dedicated to Pope St. John Paul II. The chapel is a simple one in an unassuming style, a place to stop and say a quick prayer before catching a flight. Hanging in one corner, I saw a colorful picture of a large family: a father, a pregnant mother, and many small children. This vibrant picture seemed to be there by accident. But it was no accident.

"Who are they?" I asked some other visitors to the chapel. "The Ulmas," they replied, "the family slaughtered by the Nazis in 1944 for extending hospitality to some Jews during the Second World War."

From Rzeszów I went to Przemyśl to take a train to Kyiv with some fellow journalists. We were going there to document the suffering of this senseless war, as Pope Francis has repeatedly called it.

That Przemyśl station was familiar to us, despite its name being difficult to pronounce (at least for Italians). Those halls with their chandeliers, mirrors, and somewhat retro style were featured in media images around the world when frightened Ukrainians, mainly mothers and children, poured in here starting in late February 2022. We remember the pain, the crying, but also the army of volunteers who, in a few hours and with infinite generosity, sprang into action to ease the suffering of those fleeing the horrors of the conflict.

In that station, we met the bishops and priests of the local Catholic dioceses, of the Latin and Byzantine rites, who told us about the solidarity of Poles and Ukrainians in those early days of the war in Ukraine and showed us photographs. Thanks to his excellent Italian, Fr. Witold Burda acted as interpreter.

Afterword (The Genesis of a Book) **127**

The tragic events of Ukraine begin to fill my notepad when Don Vito (as Father Witold let the Italians call him) approached with a book of old, black and white photographs, a small, folded pamphlet, and some holy cards. "Here is the history of the Ulmas," he said. "I would appreciate it if you can spend time on them, too." For the second time in a few days, I had encountered the Ulmas.

When we left Przemyśl station by night train for Kyiv, I placed Don Vito's book in my suitcase pocket, overwhelmed as I was by the tragedy of the war in Ukraine and the stories of grief I gathered in Kyiv, Kharkiv, and Izyum.

After the trip to Poland and Ukraine, I returned to work in the Vatican press office, where I follow the activities of the pope and the Holy See for the Ansa agency. On December 17, 2022, the daily bulletin of the Holy See Press Office came out at noon, with the day's official communications from the Vatican. Those communications include any promulgation of decrees by the Dicastery for the Causes of Saints. "During the Audience granted to His Eminence the Most Reverend Cardinal Marcello Semeraro, prefect of the Dicastery for the Causes of Saints, the Supreme Pontiff authorized the same Dicastery to promulgate Decrees concerning ..." A long list of names followed. Out of the sixteen stories concerning saints that day, one caught my attention: "the martyrdom of the Servants of God, Joseph and Victoria Ulma, married with their seven children; killed in hatred of the faith on March 24, 1944, at Markowa (Poland)." Pope Francis had declared that the Ulmas — the same Ulmas I had met in Poland — are martyrs and therefore blessed.

This book was created to share this story of faith and unity. This story remains, for me, inextricably connected to the war in Ukraine. I see as one the war of 1944 and the war of today: terror and solidarity; injustice and love; pain and redemption.

I contacted Fr. Paweł Rytel-Andrianik, a brilliant communicator and scholar, a polyglot, a man who is both profoundly Polish and open to the world, and, above all, a friend: "Let's make the history of the Ulmas known in Italy as well," I suggested. And he replied, "I was going to propose it to you! *Vamos!*"

And so we decided to recount the story of the nine Ulmas: Józef and Wiktoria and their children Stasia, Basia, Władziu, Franio, Antoś, and Marysia, and the seventh child in the womb. Their story has engaged and moved us for different reasons and through various personal experiences. We are sure that it will also touch the hearts of many.

(M.T.)

ACKNOWLEDGMENTS

A network of collaborations between Rome and Warsaw made this volume possible. Thanks to all those who helped, even just sending reports, making photocopies, or scanning photos and texts of the past. Without you, our work would have been more challenging.

The idea of making the Ulma family known in Italy was born from a trip organized in Poland and Ukraine to document the pain of the war but also the solidarity of many people. Special thanks go out to the ambassadors to the Holy See who facilitated the transfer of a group of Vatican journalists: Polish Ambassador Adam Mariusz Kwiatkowski and Ukrainian Ambassador Andrii Yurash. This trip introduced us to the touching story of the Ulma family, in addition to allowing us to document what happened in Ukraine in the painful months of the war and to tell the story of Poland's impressive "machine of solidarity."

We are grateful to Archbishop Stanisław Gądecki, President of the Polish Bishops' Conference, who has been engaged in Catholic-Jewish dialogue for years, for supporting the publication. Thanks to Cardinal

Stanisław Dziwisz, who supported this book as a realization of what St. John Paul II wanted in Catholic-Jewish relations. We express our gratitude to Archbishop Adam Szal, Metropolitan of Przemyśl, who asked us to promote the Ulma family abroad.

We are grateful to the Rector, Mgr. Prof. Mirosław Kalinowski, and the professors, students, and employees of the John Paul II Catholic University of Lublin for supporting this project within the work of the Abraham J. Heschel Center for Catholic-Jewish Relations.

We thank Rev. Fr. Witold Burda, postulator of the beatification process of the Ulma family, for his inspiration and contribution. We express our gratitude to Marina Olmo for her professional translation help. We are grateful to Rev. Fr. Maciej Flader and Ms. Justyna Galant for their help preparing photographic material and Dr. Witold Mędykowski for scientific consultations.

We are grateful to Sr. Amata Nowaszewska and Artur Hanula for their help preparing and promoting this book.

Last but not least, we thank the publisher of OSV, Scott P. Richert, who believed in this story from the first moment we proposed it, and Amy Richert, rights and permissions specialist for OSV, for her great help during the whole publication process.

APPENDIX I

The Markowa Museum

The Ulma family is the patron of many schools and streets in Poland. Some Catholic associations that support needy families also bear their name.

In Rzeszów, there is the Ulma Center for Family Life, and in the parish church in Brzezinka, near Oświęcim (known during the war as Auschwitz), one of the stained-glass windows depicts the Ulma family. Their image is also placed among the Polish Servants of God in the basilica in Licheń and on the front door of Przemyśl Cathedral.

The Museum of Poles Saving Jews in World War II in Poland is also named for the Ulma family. The idea of creating this museum emerged in late 2007. On June 30, 2008, the Local Parliament of the Podkarpackie province passed a unanimous resolution on establishing the museum in Markowa. After various necessary bureaucratic decisions, construction began and would last two years (October 2013 to October 2015). The museum was finally inaugurated on March 17, 2016. Its opening was attended by the President of the Republic of Poland,

Andrzej Duda, and the Ambassador of Israel to Poland, Anna Azari, as well as the President of the Polish Bishops' Conference, Archbishop Stanisław Gądecki.

There was a Mass during the inauguration of the museum in Markowa; delivering the homily was Archbishop Gądecki. After recalling that the foundation stone of the museum had been blessed by Pope Francis in 2013, Archbishop Gądecki also noted that "the Poles murdered by the Nazis for hiding and helping Jews were often individuals, but during the war, there were also situations in which entire villages were murdered for hiding Jews."[101]

The primary goal of the museum is to memorialize the heroic stance of the Poles who helped Jews during the German occupation, risking their own lives and the lives of their families. It is the first museum in Poland devoted to those who rescued Jews during the Shoah. The leading exhibition presents the known and documented cases of help provided in the present-day Podkarpackie province. There are also plans to collect testimonies and documents from the other territories of occupied Poland during World War II.

The Museum's structure is austere and minimalist, and its shape is reminiscent of a primitive house. The exhibition area is about 120 square meters. In the center is a glass cube in which the Ulma house is reproduced. The original home was located elsewhere in the village, but it no longer stands.

In front of the museum building is a square with illuminated plaques containing the names of Poles killed for rescuing Jews. A slab at the center of the court is inscribed as a memorial to the Jewish victims of the Holocaust and their anonymous Polish rescuers. The wall next to the museum building displays plaques of residents of the Podkarpackie region who helped Jews.

Fruit trees planted in the vicinity of the museum compose the Orchard of Remembrance dedicated to those Jewish people who were saved. The Orchard of Remembrance finds its roots in both Józef Ulma's passion for horticulture and the Garden of the Righteous at Yad Vashem in Jerusalem. Along the avenues of the orchard are many plaques with the names of cities, towns, and villages located in the territory of Poland in 1939, where Poles risked their lives to save Jews during the German occupation. The list includes locations where people who were awarded the title "Righteous Among the Nations" lived. In the center of the orchard is the Ulma Family Monument, unveiled on the 60th anniversary of the family's murder.

The museum's permanent exhibition is based on research carried out by the Institute of National Remembrance of the Republic of Poland, particularly the local branch in Rzeszów, which resulted in the album "Poles Rescuing Jews in the Rzeszów Region in the Years 1939–1945" by Elżbieta Rączy and Igor Witowicz, published in 2011. Another source of information for the exhibition is research conducted by Mateusz Szpytma, partly published in the book *The Righteous and Their World: Markowa in the Photographs by Józef Ulma* (Kraków, 2015).

The exhibition presents archive materials (prints, photographs, notes, documents) and is divided into the following sections:

1. Poles and Jews before 1939 in the Podkarpackie region
2. Residents of the Podkarpackie region during the German occupation
3. Poles saving Jews
4. Shelters and hiding places
5. Poles killed for helping Jews
6. The Ulma family
7. The postwar period.

In conjunction with opening of the museum in Markowa in 2016, celebrations were held at Polish embassies almost worldwide to mark this event.

The Polish ambassador to Italy at the time was Tomasz Orłowski, who, at the event organized in Rome on March 17 of that year, declared: "The Ulma family saved the world at the cost of their own lives. Their gesture saved humanity." Also present at the meeting was Ruth Dureghello, President of the Jewish Community of Rome: "The gesture that Poland makes today with the opening of the Museum of the Poles Who Saved the Jews of Markowa," she said, "is very courageous. Museums like the Shoah Museum in Rome, or like this one, have meaning if the gestures that led to their creation are remembered." Remembering "gestures and sensibilities of people who could choose and did choose is fundamental." The Ulma family "chose to save a human being, without the distinction of being Jewish or other." And finally, Dureghello reminded those present, "Memory has meaning if carried not only into the present but also into the future. We must look beyond, as the Ulmas were able to do. History has certainly changed, but we make history with our gestures."[102]

Further information on the Museum of Poles Saving Jews in World War II in Poland is available on the museum's website, muzeumulmow.pl.

The Heschel Center

A common Bible, a common past, a common future: These three elements are the pillars of the Abraham J. Heschel Center for Catholic-Jewish Relations at the John Paul II Catholic University of Lublin (KUL). The Center is a scientific and educational unit in one of the largest Catholic universities in Europe and the world. It was established on October 17, 2022, at the initiative of Rev. Prof. Mirosław Kalinowski, Rector of the Catholic University of Lublin. Its mission is to build Catholic-Jewish relations on the scientific, educational, and cultural levels internationally.

Lublin is a city with a very long history and a rich relationship between its Polish and Jewish communities. Lublin is sometimes called the "Polish Jerusalem" or "Jerusalem of the Kingdom of Poland" to indicate that it is a special place for Jews living in Poland. Before World War II, more than 42,000 Jews lived in Lublin, about one third of the local population. The tragic turning point in this long history was Nazi Germany's occupation of Poland. Nazism ultimately led to the Holocaust. The Majdanek concentration camp was organized near Lublin, and 80,000 people, most of Jewish origin, were killed there. Lublin became the first place in the General Governorate where the criminal "Action" — the planned mass extermination of the Jewish population in German-occupied Europe — began. This action led to the execution of the Ulma family, Catholics who hid Jews to protect them from deportation to extermination camps. Markowa, where the Ulmas lived and gave their lives, is less than two hundred kilometers from Lublin.

KUL's Heschel Center is dedicated to the study and promotion of the shared history of the Polish and Jewish communities, which has many beautiful aspects and examples of heroism but also dark days and tragic events, especially during World War II. Both communities were born out of deep spiritual fellowship based on the Bible. Drawing on this shared history and biblical roots, the Herschel Center aims to shape the future. It is a response to the exhortation of *Nostra Aetate*, the Second Vatican Council's Declaration on the Relation of the Church with Non-Christian Religions: "Since the spiritual patrimony common to Christians and Jews is thus so great, this sacred synod wants to foster and recommend that mutual understanding and respect which is the fruit, above all, of biblical and theological studies as well as of fraternal dialogues" (*Nostra Aetate*, no. 4).

The patron of the Center for Catholic-Jewish Relations at the Catholic University of Lublin is Rabbi Professor Abraham Joshua Heschel, an eminent theologian, philosopher, and rabbi who participated in the drafting of *Nostra Aetate*. He wrote the following on the connection between adherents of Judaism and Christianity:

> Above all, while dogmas and forms of worship are divergent, God is the same. What unites us? A commitment to the Hebrew Bible as Holy Scripture. Faith in the Creator, the God of Abraham, commitment to many of His commandments, to justice and mercy, a sense of contrition, sensitivity to the sanctity of life and to the involvement of God in history, the conviction that without the holy the good will be defeated, prayer that history may not end before the end of days, and so much more.[103]

Awareness of the shared treasures of the spirit is the foundation of the Heschel Center's work, which is to help bring believers of both religions closer together.

The Center's three categories of activity are science, education, and culture. The environment of the Catholic University of Lublin involves professional scientific staff, but also invites young people to participate in the project. The Center combines research work, commemoration of the past, education and youth involvement, and the formation of social awareness through modern media at the global level.

The Center's research activity focuses on issues of Jewish history, culture, and heritage, mainly in Poland, but also in Europe, Israel, and around the world. The mutual relations between Jewish and Catholic communities and their coexistence over the centuries are the subject of research. The Center's tasks include scientific study, documentation and archival research, scientific and educational publications, organization of scientific conferences, forums, meetings, and discussions of specific issues.

Educational activities are aimed at forming mature social attitudes, especially in young people, and developing interreligious and international dialogue. Among the forms of activities envisaged are student exchange programs between the Catholic University of Lublin and universities in Israel as well as joint projects commemorating the lives and martyrdom of people of Jewish and Polish origin, involving young people from Poland, Israel, and Europe.

An important aspect of the Center's activities is social education through media — the dissemination of knowledge and the formation of social consciousness through regular publications in the media about the results of studies and events related to the Center's activities.

The Center's cultural activities are aimed at exposing more people to Jewish culture and at cultural exchange between Jewish, Polish, and European cultures, through (for example) the organization of cultural events, cooperation with other cultural institutions and organizations, and the use of modern media in the presentation of Jewish culture and its connections with Polish and European culture.

"No religion is an island. We are all involved with one another," Rabbi Abraham J. Heschel had said. This idea inspires the activities of the Heschel Center at the Catholic University of Lublin. The institution is also inspired by the teaching and example of the University's patron, St. John Paul II, who reminded us of the important role of historical memory in shaping the future:

> Not only the shared history of Christians and Jews, but especially their dialogue must look to the future, becoming, as it were, a "memoria futuri." The memory of these sorrowful and tragic events of the past can open the path toward a renewed sense of brotherhood — the fruit of God's grace — and to working so that the seeds

infected with anti-Judaism and anti-Semitism
will never again take root in human hearts.[104]

St. John Paul II significantly changed the relationship between the Catholic Church and Judaism. Not only did he follow the directives of the Second Vatican Council, but he did so out of his own deep inner conviction. During a meeting in 1986 in the Great Roman Synagogue, he emphasized that "the Jewish religion is not a reality external to our religion, but something internal" and that the attitude toward it "is different from that of any other religion."

The Heschel Center cultivates this spiritual dimension of Catholic-Jewish relations (among others) through the joint prayers of representatives of both religions in the Lublin synagogue during Simchat Torah — the Feast of the Joy of Torah — and during the joint Advent and Hanukkah celebrations in front of the University building. In cooperation with the Archdiocese of Lublin, the Heschel Center of the Catholic University of Lublin organized a meeting dedicated to Christian-Jewish relations on the XXVI Day of Judaism in the Catholic Church in Poland.

One important event for the scientific world is the publication by the Heschel Center of a comprehensive two-volume study entitled *Wartime Rescue of Jews by the Polish Catholic Clergy* by Richard Tyndorf. The presentation of the study was accompanied by a panel discussion with scholars from Poland and Israel. Tyndorf's text documents that, during the Holocaust, aid to Jews was offered by nearly one hundred religious orders and congregations at more than five hundred locations and by more than seven hundred diocesan priests in at least 580 locations in Nazi-occupied Poland.

History requires more than the truth discovered in reliable scientific research. The remembrance of its particularly tragic episodes is also a tribute to the victims. The Heschel Center engages and involves society, particularly young people, in the commemoration of anniversaries such as that of Germany's Operation Reinhard. On the eightieth anniversary of its inception, a ceremony to commemorate the victims was held at the Majdanek concentration camp. A scientific conference on this topic was also organized at the Heschel Center headquarters. The anniversary of the "Erntefest" action in Majdanek (the largest execution in the history of German concentration and extermination camps) was also commemorated. The anniversaries of the liquidation of the Lublin and Warsaw ghettos were memorialized with the participation of numerous young people and employees of the Catholic University of Lublin.

At his general audience on October 19, 2022, Pope Francis praised the establishment of the Heschel Center by giving it his blessing. "I am pleased that the Center for Catholic-Jewish Relations has been opened in Lublin," he said. The Heschel Center's projects seek to achieve what the Holy Father wished: "I hope that the Center will help us to appreciate the common heritage not only of both religions, but of both nations."

Further information on the Abraham J. Heschel Center for Catholic-Jewish Relations is available on the center's website: heschel.kul.pl.

Prayer for Beatification
Almighty and eternal God,
we thank You for the testimony
of the heroic love
of the spouses Józef and Wiktoria with their children,
who gave their lives
to save persecuted Jews.
May their prayers and example
support families
in Christian life
and help everyone to follow

the true path of holiness.
Lord, if it is in accordance with Your will,
kindly grant me the grace ...
for which I am asking You through their
    intercession
and count them among the Blessed.
Through Christ our Lord. Amen.

APPENDIX II

Timeline

From the wedding of Józef and Wiktoria Ulma in Markowa to the establishment of the Warsaw Ghetto, and from the birth of the Polish couple's children to the outbreak of World War II, this timeline weaves the small story of the Ulmas into the large history of the war, with its wake of horror and death. Very often, history books study conflicts with only facts, dates, and political decisions. But we must never forget that at the heart of tragedies are the stories of so many real men and women, stories such as that of the Ulma family and the Jewish families they housed. In this book, we have tried to give them a face so that they do not remain cold numbers consigned to historical accounts.

1900	Józef Ulma is born on March 2 in Markowa.
1911	Józef Ulma finishes folk school.
1912	Wiktoria Ulma is born on December 10 in Markowa.
1921	Józef Ulma serves in the military.

1933	Józef Ulma is recognized in the Przeworsk District Agricultural Exhibition for his innovations in the cultivation of fruit and vegetable plants.
1935	Józef and Wiktoria Ulma are married on July 7.
1936	Józef and Wiktoria Ulma's eldest child, Stasia, is born on July 18.
1937	The Ulmas' second daughter, Basia, is born on October 6.
1938	Józef's and Wiktoria's third child, Władziu, is born on December 5.
	The Ulmas buy land in Sokal where they plan to move to expand their farming venture. (Because of the outbreak of World War II, they never moved.)
1939	A nationwide women's magazine, *Kobieta Wiejska* (*Country Woman*) comes out — a groundbreaking initiative for that era.
	Germany invades Poland on September 1, marking the beginning of the Second World War.
1940	Józef and Wiktoria's fourth child, Franio, is born on April 3.
	The Warsaw Ghetto, the largest in Europe, is established on October 16.

1941	The Ulmas's fifth child, Antoś, arrives on June 6.
	In the territories of occupied Poland, notices proliferate establishing death by shooting as the punishment for Poles who hide or help Jews.
1942	The Ulmas's youngest child, Marysia, is born on September 16.
	Probably at the end of that summer, the Didner, Grünfeld, and Goldman families ask the Ulmas to allow them hide in their home.
	Operation Reinhard is launched in Nazi-occupied territories of Poland to exterminate Polish Jews and Roma.
	On December 13, a large search operation is conducted in Markowa to find Jews who had gone into hiding.
	On December 14, the first mass shooting of Jews in Markowa takes place. Twenty-five people who had hidden in the woods on the outskirts of the village are killed after they were tracked down in the sweeping operation ordered by the German police.

1943	On February 16, the head of the Third Reich's security forces, Heinrich Himmler, orders the liquidation of the Warsaw Ghetto following an uprising by a group of its inhabitants.
	On May 16, German General Jürgen Stroop informs Berlin that the Warsaw Ghetto no longer exists.
1944	On March 24, the Germans arrive at the Ulmas's house and kill all seventeen people they find there: the eight Jews in hiding and the nine members of the Ulma family, including the baby in Wiktoria's womb.
	On September 1, Włodzimierz Leś, the Ukrainian "blue policeman" who was probably the spy who reported the Jews hiding in the Ulma house, is tried and sentenced to death by the Polskie Państwo Podziemne, the Polish Underground State.
1945	On January 11, the Ulma family's remains are moved from the garden grave at their home to the Markowa cemetery.

1947	The bodies of the Ulmas' Jewish guests, who were still in the grave in front of the home garden, are exhumed and transported to the Jagiełła cemetery.
1958	Josef Kokott, one of the perpetrators of the Ulma massacre, is sentenced to death following his trial before the Rzeszów Regional Court. (His sentence would later be commuted to life imprisonment.)
1980	Josef Kokott dies in Bytom prison.
1982	On October 10, in Saint Peter's Square, Pope John Paul II proclaims the sainthood of Maximilian Kolbe, the Franciscan priest killed in the Auschwitz concentration camp after he offered his life in exchange for that of a family man.
1994	The first session of the diocesan inquiry for the beatification and canonization of Servants of God Fr. Henryk Szuman and 121 companions, martyrs from World War II, is held on September 29.
1995	The title of Righteous Among the Nations is bestowed on Józef and Wiktoria Ulma.

1999	In a celebration in Warsaw on June 13, Pope John Paul II proclaimed as blessed 108 Polish martyrs who were victims of the Nazis, including three bishops.
2003	On September 17, the Archdiocese of Przemyśl initiates the beatification process for the entire Ulma family.
2004	A monument dedicated to the Ulma family is unveiled in Markowa.
2010	President of the Republic of Poland Lech Kaczyński decorates the entire Ulma family with the Commander's Cross of the Order of Polonia Restituta.
2011	The diocesan beatification process for Servant of God Henryk Szuman and 88 Companions, martyrs from World War II, ends on May 24.
2016	In March, the Museum of the Poles Who Saved Jews, named after the Ulma family, opens in Markowa.
	On July 29, during a visit to the Auschwitz concentration camp, Pope Francis learns about the story of the Ulma family from Markowa parish priest Fr. Stanisław Ruszała.

Appendix II **151**

2017	On February 20, the cause of Servants of God Józef and Wiktoria Ulma and their seven children is separated from the beatification process of Servant of God Henryk Szuman and 88 Companions. This is granted by the Dicastery for the Causes of Saints at the request of the Archbishop of Przemyśl, Monsignor Adam Szal, allowing for an independent beatification process for the Ulmas.
2018	March 24, the day the Ulma family was murdered, is marked for the first time in Poland as an annual National Day of Remembrance for Poles Who Saved Jews Under German Occupation.
	At his general audience on November 28, Pope Francis cites the Ulma family as an "example of fidelity to God and His commandments."
2020	The *Positio*, the document that gathers all the testimonies and documents about the Ulma family in the beatification and canonization process, is finalized in July.
2021	On February 16 the *Positio* on the Ulmas is submitted to historians for evaluation.

2022	On February 22, the *Positio* regarding the beatification of the Ulma family is submitted to the Theological Consultors for review.
	On December 17, the conclusions of the cardinals and bishops are submitted by Cardinal Marcello Semeraro, prefect of the Dicastery for the Causes of Saints, to the Holy Father for final approval, during an audience in which Pope Francis approves the decree on the martyrdom of the Ulmas.
2023	The exhumation and canonical recognition of the Ulma family's remains takes place in the Markowa parish cemetery from March 30 to April 1 (standard practice for all beatifications).
	On Sunday, September 10, in Markowa, all members of the Ulma family are beatified: Józef and Wiktoria, along with their children Stasia, Basia, Władziu, Franio, Antoś, Marysia, and the little unnamed child.
	The national pilgrimage of the relics of the Ulma family begins on September 24, during the XXXIX Pilgrimage to Jasna Góra for couples and families. The relics visit the Archdiocese of Częstochowa before being taken to the other dioceses in Poland.

NOTES

1. Editor's note: Louis Martin and Azélie-Marie Guérin were proclaimed saints on October 18, 2015, by Pope Francis, with a celebration in Saint Peter's Square.

2. Editor's note: The Holy Innocents were the children killed in Bethlehem at Herod's behest.

3. Editor's note: Salvo Rosario Antonio D'Acquisto was a vice brigadier in the Carabinieri Corps and was awarded the Gold Medal for Military Valor for sacrificing himself on September 23, 1943, to save a group of civilians during a Nazi roundup during World War II. In 1983 the Military Ordinariate opened the cause for beatification and canonization. In 1991 the acts were forwarded to the Congregation (now Dicastery) for the Causes of Saints.

4. For the history of Markowa, see J. Półćwiartek (ed.), *Z dziejów wsi Markowa*, Rzeszów, Poland, 1993; W. Blajer, J. Tejchma (ed.), *Markowa – sześć wieków tradycji. Z dziejów społeczeństwa i kultury*, Markowa, Poland, 2005; J. Tejchma, *Dawniej. O ludziach i czasach w Markowej*, Kraków, Poland, 2019.

5. The museum dedicated to the Ulma family and to the Jews who were killed with them can be visited online at www.muzeumulmow.pl. See also the Archdiocese of Przemyśl website dedicated to them: www.ulmowie.pl.

6. One of the historians who has written the most on the history of the Ulmas is Mateusz Szpytma, a Markowa native. See M. Szpytma, *The Risk of Survival. The Rescue of the Jews by the Poles and*

the Tragic Consequences for the Ulma Family from Markowa, IPN, Warsaw-Kraków, 2009; M. Szpytma, *Sprawiedliwi i ich świat. Markowa w fotografii Józefa Ulmy*, IPN, Kraków, 2015; M. Szpytma, "The Ulma Family: A Symbol of the Poles Murdered for Helping Jews," in: W. Wierzbieniec, E. Rączy (ed.), *Righteous Among Nations: The Scope and Form of Help to Jews in East and Central Europe During Occupation by Third Reich*, Jarosław, Poland, 2014, 19–70.

7. Interview with the postulator of the cause for beatification, Fr. Witold Burda, on the channel *Sacre questioni*, May 30, 2021, https://www.youtube.com/watch?v=U6UCrhjQla4.

8. Mt 25:14–30.

9. Interview with Stanisława Kuźniar at eKai.pl, March 23, 2023, https://www.ekai.pl/stanislawa-kuzniar-nikt-nie-mogl-uwierzyc-ze-niemcy-nie-oszczedzili-nawet-dzieci-ulmow/.

10. Ibid.,

11. Interview with Fr. Witold Burda on the channel Sacre questioni, May 30, 2021, https://www.youtube.com/watch?v=U6UCrhjQla4.

12. M. E. Szulikowska, *Wiktoria Ulma. Opowieść o miłości*, Kraków, 2023.

13. Interview with Maria Elżbieta Szulikowska at the Opoka portal, May 18, 2023.

14. Interview with Fr. Witold Burda, Sacre questioni, June 10, 2021, https://www.youtube.com/watch?v=U6UCrhjQla4.

15. Interview with Stanisława Kuźniar, March 23, 2023.

16. Message published on the Vicenza diocese's website: https://www.diocesivicenza.it/wd-document/auguri-natalizi-del-vescovo-di-

vicenza-2022-un-bambino-e-nato-per-noi/.

17. K. Kopera, *Losy Żydów z Markowej*, Markowa, 2020, 38.

18. Ibid., 38–48.

19. Ibid., 42.

20. For more information on life in the community of Łańcut, see the memoirs of the town's inhabitants: N. Kudisch, M. Walzer M. (ed.) *Lancut. Hayeha vehurbana shel kehila Yehudit*, Tel Aviv, 1963.

21. *Pod Pręgierz*, "Nowy Dziennik," January 15, 2022, 3. Citation from Kopera, *Losy Żydów z Markowej*, 43, note 99. This was in response to the fact that the Jewish community of Łańcut (kahal), was dissolved and the government appointed a commissioner and council composed of Zionist representatives, and Orthodox Jews did not want them to be part of it.

22. Kopera, *Losy Żydów z Markowej*, 46.

23. As mentioned earlier, Mechel Goldman and Chana Rosengarten did not legalize their relationship for a long time, so their children bore their mother's surname, Rosengarten.

24. Kopera, *Losy Żydów z Markowej*, 46.

25. Ibid., 46–47.

26. Questionnaire completed by Mechel Goldman as part of the candidacy of persons practicing medical professions in the General Government. Cited in Kopera, *Losy Żydów z Markowej*, 45.

27. M. Szpytma, *Sprawiedliwi i ich świat. Markowa w fotografii Józefa Ulmy*, 31.

28. Ibid., 30

29. Ibid., 31.

30. *Rodzina Ulmów, Droga ku świętości*, Kraków 2023, 9.

31. Cf. B. Kirshenblatt-Gimblett, A. Polonsky (ed.), *Polin. 1000 Years History of Polish Jews. A Guide*, Museum of the History of Polish Jews, Warsaw, 2014; A. Cała, H. Węgrzynek, G. Zalewska, *Historia i kultura Żydów Polskich. Słownik*, Warszawa 2000; A. Polonsky, *The Jews in Poland and Russia*, I: 1350–1881, The Littman Library of Jewish Civilization, Oxford and Portland, OR, 2010.

32. Antony Polonsky, *The Jews in Poland and Russia*, I: 1350–1881, 68.

33. Ibid., 68–90.

34. Kopera, *Losy Żydów z Markowej*, 9–21.

35. Cf. B. Kirshenblatt-Gimblett, Antony Polonsky (ed.), *Polin. 1000 Years History of Polish Jews. A Guide*, 37.

36. "Nuremberg Laws on Reich Citizenship, September 15, 1935," Reichgesetzblatt, I, 1935, 1146, in: Y. Arad, Y. Gutman et al. (ed.), *Documents on the Holocaust: Selected Sources on the Destruction of the Jews of Germany and Austria, Poland and the Soviet Union*, Yad Vashem, Jerusalem, 1987, 77.

37. W. Wichert, "*Niemiecki system okupacyjny na ziemiach polskich w latach 1939-1945. Zarys problematyki*," in T. Domański, A. Gontarek (ed.), *Stan badań nad pomocą Żydom na ziemiach polskich pod okupacją niemiecką — przegląd piśmiennictwa*, IPN, Warszawa-Kielce, Poland, 2022, 28–82.

38. On October 30, 1939, Himmler issued a decree as Reich Commissioner for the Consolidation of German Nationhood (Reichskommissar für die Festigung deutschen Volkstums - RKFDV) ordering the expulsion of the Polish and Jewish populations from areas annexed to the German Reich. A. Głowacka-Penczyńska, T. Kawski, W. Mędyko-

wski, *The First to be Destroyed: The Jewish Community of Kleczew and the Beginning of the Final Solution*, Tuvia Horev (ed.), Boston, 2015, 149.

39. Cf. Polonsky, *The Jews in Poland and Russia*, III: 1914 to 2008, The Littman Library of Jewish Civilization, Oxford and Portland, OR, 2012, 361–412, 434; M. Grądzka-Rejak, A. Namysło, "Prawodawstwo niemieckie wobec Polaków i Żydów na terenie Generalnego Gubernatorstwa oraz ziem wcielonych do III Rzeszy. Analiza porównawcza," in T. Domański, A. Gontarek (ed.), *Stan badań nad pomocą Żydom na ziemiach polskich pod okupacją niemiecką — przegląd piśmiennictwa*, 83–110.

40. From a Speech by Frank on the Extermination of the Jews, December 16, 1941, https://www.yadvashem.org/docs/frank-speech-on-jews-extermination.html.

41. Cf. T. Prekerowa, Zarys dziejów Żydów w Polsce w latach 1939–1945, Warsaw, 1992, 11-79.

42. Instructions (Schnellbrief) by Heydrich on policy and operations concerning Jews in the occupied territories, September 21, 1939, NMT PS-3363, in Y. Arad, Y. Gutman et al. (ed.), Documents on the Holocaust: Selected Sources on the Destruction of the Jews of Germany and Austria, Poland and the Soviet Union, 173–178.

43. Polonsky, *The Jews in Poland and Russia*, III: 1914 to 2008, 368, 374–376, S. Aronson, P. Longerich, "Final Solution: Preparation and Implementation": W. Laqueur, J. T. Baumel (ed.), *The Holocaust Encyclopedia*, New Heaven, London, 2001, 184–198.

44. Polonsky, *The Jews in Poland and Russia*, III: 1914 to 2008, 371–376.

45. Cf. G. P. Megargee (ed.), *Encyclopedia of Camps and Ghettos 1933–1945*, vol. II, part A-B: Ghettos in German-Occupied Eastern Europe, The United States Holocaust Memorial Museum, Bloomington, IN, and Indianapolis, 2012.

46. Polonsky, *The Jews in Poland and Russia*, III: 1914 to 2008, 413–436.

47. Third regulation on the restriction of residency in the General Government of October 15, 1941, Verordnungsblatt für das Generalgouvernements, 1941, no. 99, 595, in Frank Hans, *Okupacja i ruch oporu w dzienniku Hansa Franka 1939–1945*, vol. I, Warsaw, 1970, 428.

48. *Protocol of the Wannsee Conference*, January 20, 1942, NMT NG-2586-G, Y. Arad, Y. Gutman et al. (ed.), *Documents on the Holocaust: Selected Sources on the Destruction of the Jews of Germany and Austria, Poland and the Soviet Union*, 249–261.

49. Megargee (ed.), *Encyclopedia of Camps and Ghettos 1933-1945*, vol. I, part A-B: *Early Camps, Youth Camps, and Concentration Camps and Subcamps under the SS-Business Administration Main Office (WVHA)*.

50. S. Krakowski, *Chełmno. A small village in Europe: the first Nazi Mass Extermination Camp*, Jerusalem, 2009.

51. Cf. E. Kopówka, P. Rytel-Andrianik, *Dam im imię na wieki (Iz 56,5). Polacy z okolic Treblinki ratujący Żydów*, Oxford and Treblinka, Poland, 2011, 35–124.

52. Y. Arad, *Belzec, Sobibor, Treblinka: The Operation Reinhard Death Camps*, Bloomington 1999; S. Lehnstaedt, R. Traba (ed.), *Die "Aktion Reinhardt". Geschichte und Gedenken*, Berlin 2019; T. Głowiński, S. Lehnstaedt, W. Mędykowski, *As If We Had Never Existed*.

Extermination of Jews as a Part of the German Aktion "Reinhardt", Warsaw, 2022.

53. W. Lenarczyk, D. Libionka (ed.), *Erntefest 3-4 listopada 1943 — zapomniany epizod Zagłady*, Państwowe Muzeum na Majdanku, Lublin, Poland, 2009.

54. Polonsky, *The Jews in Poland and Russia*, III: 1914 to 2008, 418.

55. W. Materski, T. Szarota (ed.), *Polska 1939–1945. Straty osobowe i ofiary represji pod dwiema okupacjami*, IPN, Warsaw, 2009.

56. Polonsky, *The Jews in Poland and Russia*, III: 1914 to 2008, 368.

57. Editor's note: The Aryan side was the part of the city outside of the ghettos, where the non-Jewish population lived.

58. Antony Polonsky, "Próba podziękowania," in E. Kopówka, P. Rytel-Andrianik, *Dam im imię na wieki (Iz 56,5). Polacy z okolic Treblinki ratujący Żydów*, 10. L'Autore fornisce questi dati anche in A. Polonsky, *The Jews in Poland and Russia*, III: 1914 to 2008, 460. Regarding the number of Jews who survived the war, see Polonsky, *The Jews in Poland and Russia*, III: 1914 to 2008, 436: "By the end of 1942 most of Polish Jewry had been murdered. … By the time of liberation around 15,500 Polish Jews were still alive in various concentration camps and between 30,000 and 50,000 were in hiding. Perhaps another 5,000 were fighting in the various partisan movements."

59. Polonsky, "Próba podziękowania," in E. Kopówka, P. Rytel-Andrianik, *Dam im imię na wieki (Iz 56,5). Polacy z okolic Treblinki ratujący Żydów*, 11.

60. Y. Gutman, "Contribution to Discussion on Ethical Problems

of the Holocaust in Poland," in A. Polonsky (ed.), *My Brother's Keeper? Recent Polish Debates on the Holocaust*, London 1990, 296–298

61. R. Tyndorf, Z. Zieliński, *Wartime Rescue of Jews by the Polish Catholic Clergy. The Testimony of Survivors and Rescuers*, Vol. 1–2, Lublin 2023. Tutto il libro in open access: https://repozytorium.kul.pl/handle/20.500.12153/4756.

62. Polonsky, "Próba podziękowania" in E. Kopówka, P. Rytel-Andrianik, *Dam im imię na wieki (Iz 56,5). Polacy z okolic Treblinki ratujący Żydów*, 9.

63. *Rada Pomocy Żydom w Polsce ("Żegota"). Wspomnienia centralnych i terenowych działaczy RPŻ*, Warsaw, 1968; M. Arczyński, W. Balcerak, *Kryptonim "Żegota." Konspiracyjna Rada Pomocy Żydom 1942–1945*, Mińsk-Toronto-Warszawa 2009; *"Żegota" Rada Pomocy Żydom 1942–1945. Wybór dokumentów*, ed. A. K. Kunert (ed.), Warsaw, 2002; T. Prekerowa, *Konspiracyjna Rada Pomocy Żydom w Warszawie 1942–1945*, Warsaw, 2019.

64. J. Kumoch, M. Maniewska, J. Uszyński, B. Zygmunt et al., *Lista Ładosia. Spis osób, na których nazwiska w okresie II wojny światowej zostały wystawione paszporty latynoamerykańskie przez Poselstwo RP i organizacje żydowskie w Szwajcarii*, Warsaw, 2019.

65. A. Gontarek, "Dyplomacja polska a pomoc udzielana Żydom na ziemiach polskich pod okupacją niemiecką w latach 1939–1943 – stan badań", in: T. Domański, A. Gontarek (ed.), *Stan badań nad pomocą Żydom na ziemiach polskich pod okupacją niemiecką – przegląd piśmiennictwa*, 113–174.

66. Książki są dostępne online tutaj: https://libguides.nypl.org/yizkorbooks.

67. Cf. M. Adamczyk-Garbowska, A. Kopciowski, A. Trzciński, *Tam był kiedyś mój dom… Księgi pamięci gmin żydowskich*, Lublin, Poland, 2009. Często na temat jednej miejscowości jest kilka książek.

68. *The Encyclopedia of the Righteous Among the Nations. Rescuers of Jews during the Holocaust in Poland*, I. Gutman (ed.), Jerusalem, 2004.

69. https://www.yadvashem.org/righteous/statistics.html.

70. For the history of Markowa, cf. J. Półćwiartek (ed.), *Z dziejów wsi Markowa*; W. Blajer, J. Tejchma (ed.), *Markowa – sześć wieków tradycji. Z dziejów społeczeństwa i kultury*; J. Tejchma, *Dawniej. O ludziach i czasach w Markowej*.

71. O. Maciuk, "Markowa w świetle dokumentów z archiwów lwowskich," in W. Blajer, J. Tejchma (ed.), *Markowa – sześć wieków tradycji. Z dziejów społeczeństwa i kultury*, 35. One of the first mentions of Markowa came in the year 1384.

72. Kopera, *Losy Żydów z Markowej*, 9–21.

73. S. Spector, G. Wigoder (ed.), *The Encyclopedia of Jewish Life Before and During the Holocaust*, vol. II, New York and Jerusalem, 2001, 796.

74. S. Dobosz, "W walce z okupantem hitlerowskim," in J. Półćwiartek (ed.), *Z dziejów wsi Markowa*, s. 96.

75. Interview with Fr. Witold Burda, "Sacre Questioni," June 10, 2021.

76. "Józef Ulma, Wiktoria Ulma," in *Polacy Ratujący Żydów w czasie Zagłady. Przywracanie pamięci / Poles Who Rescued Jews during the Holocaust. Recalling Forgotten History*, Kancelaria Prezydenta Rzeczypospolitej Polskiej / Chancellery of the President of the Republic

of Poland, Łódź, Poland, 2009, 144–145.

77. Z. Wawszczak, "Józef Ulma (1900–1944)" in J. Półćwiartek (ed.), *Z dziejów wsi Markowa*, s. 463.

78. M. Schudrich, "They Saved More Than Just Lives" in *Polacy Ratujący Żydów w czasie Zagłady. Przywracanie pamięci / Poles Who Rescued Jews during the Holocaust. Recalling Forgotten History*, Kancelaria Prezydenta Rzeczypospolitej Polskiej / Chancellery of the President of the Republic of Poland, Łódź, Poland, 2009, 10.

79. Interview with Stanisława Kuźniar, eKai.pl, March 23, 2023, https://www.ekai.pl/stanislawa-kuzniar-nikt-nie-mogl-uwierzyc-ze-niemcy-nie-oszczedzili-nawet-dzieci-ulmow/.

80. M. Szpytma, *The Risk of Survival*, 79.

81. Ibid.

82. Ibid.

83. Archives of the Institute of National Remembrance (IPN), Rzeszów Section, IPN Rz 107/1608, Proceedings concerning Józef Kokott, t. II, Minutes of the hearing of the witness Teofila Kielara, Rzeszów, Poland, March 21, 1958, sheet 47.

84. Archives of the Institute of National Remembrance (IPN), Rzeszów Section, IPN Rz 107/1608, Proceedings concerning Józef Kokott, t. I, Minutes of the hearing of Franciszek Szylar, March 1, 1958, sheet 297.

85. Błogosławione owoce at niedziela.pl, March 15, 2023, https://www.niedziela.pl/artykul/164447/nd/Blogoslawione-owoce.

86. A. Duda, President of Poland, Letter at Abraham Segal's funeral, https://www.thefirstnews.com/article/polish-presidents-letter-read-out-at-abraham-segals-funeral-5736.

87. Dobosz, "W walce z okupantem hitlerowskim", in: J. Półćwiartek (ed.), *Z dziejów wsi Markowa*, s. 95.

88. Ibid.

89. "*Papa: ricorda famiglia polacca sterminata per aiuto a ebrei*," Ansa, November 28, 2018.

90. "*Papa: minaccia antisemitismo è una miccia che va spenta*," Ansa, November 9, 2021.

91. S. Gądecki, "*Bądź doskonały we wszystkich próbach. Otwarcie Muzeum Ulmów (Markowa – 17.03.2016),*" https://episkopat.pl/homilia-badz-doskonaly-we-wszystkich-probach-otwarcie-muzeum-ulmow-markowa-17-03-2016/.

92. Statements collected by Fr. Maciej Flader, ulmowie.pl, April 30, 2023.

93. "*Józef e Wiktoria Ulma e i loro sette figli*," Dicastery for the Causes of Saints, causesanti.va.

94. I. Sambucci, "*Gli Ulma presto beati, il postulatore: 'Una famiglia martire per amore,*'" Vatican News, December 21, 2022, https://www.vaticannews.va/it/chiesa/news/2022-12/famiglia-ulma-beati-intervista-postulatore-polonia.html.

95. Interview with Fr. Witold Burda, "Sacre Questioni," June 10, 2021, https://www.youtube.com/watch?v=U6UCrhjQla4.

96. "Poland's Ulma Family, Murdered By Nazis, Is Present in Life, Suffering of Maryland Family," OSV News, March 27, 2023, https://www.osvnews.com/2023/03/27/polands-ulma-family-murdered-by-nazis-is-present-in-life-suffering-of-maryland-family/.

97. F.-M. Léthel, "*Insieme per sempre. Il riconoscimento del martirio di Józef e Wiktoria Ulma e dei loro sette figli uccisi dai na-*

zisti nel 1944," https://www.osservatoreromano.va/it/news/2023-03/quo-067/insieme-per-sempre.html.

98. Ibid.

99. Ibid.

100. http://kaplica-pamieci.pl.

101. "*Siate perfetti in tutte le prove*," homily of Monsignor Stanisław Gądecki on March 17, 2016, https://episkopat.pl/homilia-badz-doskonaly-we-wszystkich-probach-otwarcie-muzeum-ulmow-markowa-17-03-2016/.

102. "*Polonia: a Markowa museo dei polacchi che salvarono Ebrei*," Ansa, March 17, 2016, https://www.ansa.it/nuova_europa/it/notizie/nazioni/polonia/2016/03/18/polonia-a-markowa-museo-dei-polacchi-che-salvarono-ebrei_083f999a-fe34-4b06-9d1f-9fb1c653edf7.html.

103. A. J. Heschel, "No Religion is an Island," in *No Religion is an Island. Abraham Joshua Heschel and Interreligious Dialogue*, ed. H. Kasimov and B. L. Sherwin, trans. M. Kapera (Kraków, 2005), p. 36.

104. General Audience, April 28, 1999.

BIBLIOGRAPHY

Adamczyk-Garbowska, M., A. Kopciowski, and A. Trzciński, *Tam był kiedyś mój dom... Księgi pamięci gmin żydowskich*, Lublin, Poland, 2009.

Arad, Y., *Belzec, Sobibor, Treblinka: The Operation Reinhard Death Camps*, Bloomington, Indiana, 1999.

Archives of the Institute of National Remembrance (IPN), Rzeszów Section, IPN Rz 107/1608, 1958.

Arczyński, M., and W Balcerak, *Kryptonim "Żegota." Konspiracyjna Rada Pomocy Żydom 1942–1945*, Mińsk-Toronto-Warsaw, 2009.

Blajer, W., and J. Tejchma (ed.), *Markowa – sześć wieków tradycji. Z dziejów społeczeństwa i kultury*, Markowa 2005.

Cała, A., H. Węgrzynek, and G. Zalewska, *Historia i kultura Żydów Polskich. Słownik*, Warsaw, 2000.

Dobosz, S., "W walce z okupantem hitlerowskim", in J. Półćwiartek (ed.), *Z dziejów wsi Markowa*, Rzeszów, Poland, 1993, s. 95–96.

Głowacka-Penczyńska A., T. Kawski, and W. Mędykowski, *The First to Be Destroyed: The Jewish Community of Kleczew and the Beginning of the Final Solution*, Tuvia Horev (ed.), Boston 2015.

Głowiński, T., S. Lehnstaedt, and W. Mędykowski, *As If We Had Never Existed. Extermination of Jews as a Part of the German Aktion "Reinhardt,"* Warsaw, 2022.

Gontarek, A., "*Dyplomacja polska a pomoc udzielana Żydom na ziemiach polskich pod okupacją niemiecką w latach 1939–1943 – stan badań,*" in Domański, Tomasz, and Alicja Gontarek (ed.), *Stan badań nad pomocą Żydom na ziemiach polskich pod okupacją niemiecką - przegląd piśmiennictwa*, IPN, Warszawa-Kielce, Poland, 2022, 113–174.

Grądzka-Rejak, M., and A. Namysło, "*Prawodawstwo niemieckie wobec Polaków I Żydów na terenie Generalnego Gubernatorstwa oraz ziem wcielonych do III Rzeszy. Analiza porównawcza,*" in Domański and Gontarek (ed.), *Stan badań nad pomocą Żydom na ziemiach polskich pod okupacją niemiecką – przegląd piśmiennictwa*, IPN, Warszawa-Kielce, Poland, 2022, 83–110.

Gutman, I. (ed.), *The Encyclopedia of the Righteous Among the Nations. Rescuers of Jews during the Holocaust in Poland*, Jerusalem, 2004.

Gutman, Y., "Contribution to Discussion on Ethical Problems of the Holocaust in Poland," in Polonsky, A. (ed.), *My Brother's Keeper? Recent Polish Debates on the Holocaust,* London, 1990, 296–298.

Instructions (Schnellbrief) by Heydrich on policy and operations concerning Jews in the occupied territories, September 21, 1939, NMT PS-3363, in Arad, Y., and Y.Gutman, et al. (ed.), *Documents on the Holocaust: Selected Sources on the Destruction of the Jews of Germany and Austria, Poland and the Soviet Union*, Yad Vashem, Jerusalem 1987, 173–178.

"Józef Ulma, Wiktoria Ulma" in *Polacy Ratujący Żydów w czasie Zagłady. Przywracanie pamięci / Poles Who Rescued Jews during the Holocaust. Recalling Forgotten History*, Kancelaria Prezydenta Rzeczypospolitej Polskiej / Chancellery of the President of the Republic of Poland, 144–145.

Kirshenblatt-Gimblett, B. (ed.), *Polin. 1000 Years History of Polish Jews. A Guide,* Museum of the History of Polish Jews, Warsaw, 2014.

Kopera, K., *Losy Żydów z Markowej*, Markowa, Poland, 2020.

Kopówka, E., and P.Rytel-Andrianik, *Dam im imię na wieki (Iz 56,5). Polacy z okolic Treblinki ratujący Żydów*, Oxford and Treblinka, Poland, 2011.

Krakowski, S., *Chełmno. A Small Village in Europe: the First Nazi Mass Extermination Camp*, Jerusalem, 2009.

Kudisch, N., and M. Walzer-Fass (ed.) *Lancut. Hayeha vehurbana shel kehila Yehudit*, Tel Aviv, 1963.

Kumoch, J., M. Maniewska, J. Uszyński, and B. Zygmunt, et al., *Lista Ładosia. Spis osób, na których nazwiska w okresie*

II wojny światowej zostały wystawione paszporty latyno-amerykańskie przez Poselstwo RP i organizacje żydowskie w Szwajcarii, Warsaw, 2019.

Kunert, A. K. (ed.), *"Żegota" Rada Pomocy Żydom 1942–1945. Wybór dokumentów*, Warsaw, 2002.

Lehnstaedt, S., and R. Traba (ed.), *Die "Aktion Reinhardt." Geschichte und Gedenken*, Berlin, 2019.

Lenarczyk, W., and D. Libionka (ed.), *Erntefest 3–4 listopada 1943 – zapomniany epizod Zagłady*, Państwowe Muzeum na Majdanku, Lublin, Poland, 2009.

Maciuk O., "*Markowa w świetle dokumentów z archiwów lwowskich*," in Blajer, W., and J. Tejchma (ed.), *Markowa – sześć wieków tradycji. Z dziejów społeczeństwa i kultury*, Markowa 2005, 35–41.

Materski, W., and T. Szarota (ed.), *Polska 1939–1945. Straty osobowe i ofiary represji pod dwiema okupacjami*, IPN, Warsaw, 2009.

Megargee, G. P. (ed.), *Encyclopedia of Camps and Ghettos 1933–1945*, vol. I, part A-B: *Early Camps, Youth Camps, and Concentration Camps and Subcamps under the SS-Business Administration Main Office (WVHA)*, The United States Holocaust Memorial Museum, Bloomington, Indiana, and Indianapolis, 2012.

———, *Encyclopedia of Camps and Ghettos 1933–1945*, vol. II, part A-B: *Ghettos in German-Occupied Eastern Europe*,

The United States Holocaust Memorial Museum, Bloomington, Indiana, and Indianapolis, 2012.

"Nuremberg Laws on Reich Citizenship, September 15, 1935," Reichgesetzblatt, I, 1935, 1146, in Arad, Y., Y. Gutman, et al. (ed.), *Documents on the Holocaust: Selected Sources on the Destruction of the Jews of Germany and Austria, Poland and the Soviet Union*, 77.

Polonsky, A., "Próba podziękowania," in Kopówka, E., and P. Rytel-Andrianik, *Dam im imię na wieki (Iz 56,5). Polacy z okolic Treblinki ratujący Żydów*, Oxford and Treblinka, Poland, 2011, 10.

---------, *The Jews in Poland and Russia, I: 1350–1881*, The Littman Library of Jewish Civilization, Oxford and Portland, Oregon, 2010.

---------, *The Jews in Poland and Russia, III: 1914 to 2008*, The Littman Library of Jewish Civilization, Oxford and Portland, Oregon, 2012.

Półćwiartek, J. (ed.), *Z dziejów wsi Markowa*, Rzeszów, Poland, 1993.

Prekerowa, T., *Konspiracyjna Rada Pomocy Żydom w Warszawie 1942-1945*, Warsaw, 2019.

---------, *Zarys dziejów Żydów w Polsce w latach 1939–1945*, Warsaw, 1992.

Protocol of the Wannsee Conference, January 20, 1942, NMT NG-2586-G, Arad, Y., Y. Gutman, et al. (ed.), *Documents* on the Holocaust: Selected Sources on the Destruction of the Jews of Germany and Austria, Poland and the Soviet Union, Yad Vashem, 249–261.

Rada Pomocy Żydom w Polsce ("Żegota"). Wspomnienia centralnych i terenowych działaczy RPŻ, Warsaw, 1968.

Rodzina Ulmów, Droga ku świętości, Kraków, Poland, 2023.

Schudrich, M., "They Saved More Than Just Lives," in Polacy ratujący Żydów w czasie Zagłady. Przywracanie pamięci / Polacchi che salvarono gli ebrei durante l'Olocausto. Ricordando la storia dimenticata, Kancelaria Prezydenta Rzeczypospolitej Polskiej / Chancellory of the President of the Republic of Poland, Łódź, Poland, 2009, 10.

Spector, S., and G. Wigoder (ed.), The Encyclopedia of Jewish Life Before and During the Holocaust, vol. II, New York and Jerusalem, 2001.

Szpytma, M, Sprawiedliwi i ich świat. Markowa w fotografii Józefa Ulmy, IPN, Kraków, Poland, 2015.

———, The Risk of survival. The Rescue of the Jews by the Poles and the Tragic Consequences for the Ulma Family from Markowa, IPN, Warsaw-Kraków, 2009.

———, "The Ulma Family: A Symbol of the Poles Murdered for Helping Jews," in Wierzbieniec, W., and E. Rączy (ed.), Righteous Among Nations: The Scope and Form of Help to Jews in East and Central Europe During Occupation by Third Reich, Jarosław, Poland, 2014, 19–70.

Szpytma, M., and J. Szarek, *Rodzina Ulmów*, Kraków 2018.

Szulikowska, M. E., *Wiktoria Ulma. Opowieść o miłości*, Kraków, Poland, 2023.

Tejchma, J., *Dawniej. O ludziach i czasach w Markowej*, Kraków 2019.

Tyndorf, R., and Z. Zieliński Z., *Wartime Rescue of Jews by the Polish Catholic Clergy. The Testimony of Survivors and Rescuers*, Vol. 1–2, Lublin, Poland, 2023.

Verordnungsblatt für das Generalgouvernements, 1941, nr 99, 595, in Frank Hans, *Okupacja i ruch oporu w dzienniku Hansa Franka 1939–1945*, vol. I, Warsaw, 1970, 428.

Wawszczak, Z., "Józef Ulma (1900–1944)," in Półćwiartek, J. (ed.), *Z dziejów wsi Markowa*, s. 463.

Wichert, W., "*Niemiecki system okupacyjny na ziemiach polskich w latach 1939-1945. Zarys problematyki*" in Domański, T., and A. Gontarek (ed.), *Stan badań nad pomocą Żydom na ziemiach polskich pod okupacją niemiecką — przegląd piśmiennictwa*, IPN, Warszawa-Kielce, Poland, 2022, 28–82.

Websites

"Błogosławione owoce," niedziela.pl, March 15, 2023, https://www.niedziela.pl/artykul/164447/nd/Blogoslawione-owoce.

Burda, W., Interview with the Sacre questioni portal, May 30,

2021, https://www.youtube.com/watch?v=U6UCrhjQla4.

Dicastery for the Causes of Saints, "*Józef e Wiktoria Ulma e i loro sette figli*," https://www.causesanti.va/it/santi-e-beati/jozef-e-wiktoria-ulma-e-sette-figli.html.

Diocese of Vicenza, Message published on the website by the diocese, https://www.diocesivicenza.it/wd-document/auguri-natalizi-del-vescovo-di-vicenza-2022-un-bambino-e-nato-per-noi/.

Duda, A., President of Poland, Letter at Abraham Segal's funeral, https://www.thefirstnews.com/article/polish-presidents-letter-read-out-at-abraham-segals-funeral-5736.

Flader, M. don, Dichiarazioni raccolte, ulmowie.pl, April 30, 2023.

Gądecki, S. arciv., "*Siate perfetti in tutte le prove*," homily, March 17, 2016, https://episkopat.pl/homilia-badz-doskonaly-we-wszystkich-probach-otwarcie-muzeum-ulmow-markowa-17-03-2016 .

———, "Bądź doskonały we wszystkich próbach. Otwarcie Muzeum Ulmów (Markowa – 17.03.2016)," https://episkopat.pl/homilia-badz-doskonaly-we-wszystkich-probach-otwarcie-muzeum-ulmow-markowa-17-03-2016/.

Krajewski, K. kard., Homily of the Mass at the Tomb of John Paul II in Saint Peter's Basilica, March 30 2023, https://

stacja7.pl/zwatykanu/kard-krajewski-o-janie-pawle-ii-takich-prorokow-swiat-zabija-i-poniewiera-nimi-takze-po-smierci/.

Kuźniar, S., Interview at eKai.pl portal, March 23, 2023, https://www.ekai.pl/stanislawa-kuzniar-nikt-nie-mogl-uwierzyc-ze-niemcy-nie-oszczedzili-nawet-dzieci-ulmow/.

Léthel, F.-M., "*Insieme per sempre. Il riconoscimento del martirio di Józef e Wiktoria Ulma e dei loro sette figli uccisi dai nazisti nel 1944*," https://www.osservatoreromano.va/it/news/2023-03/quo-067/insieme-per-sempre.html.

Names and Numbers of Righteous Among the Nations - per Country and Ethnic Origin, as of January 1, 2022, https://www.yadvashem.org/righteous/statistics.html.

Notiziario del 28-11-2018, https://www.youtube.com/watch?v=j3sOf9LucDI.

"*Papa ricorda famiglia polacca sterminata per aiuto a ebrei*," Ansa, November 28, 2018.

"*Papa: minaccia antisemitismo è una miccia che va spenta*," Ansa, November 9, 2021.

"Poland's Ulma Family, Murdered By Nazis, Is Present In Life, Suffering Of Maryland Family," OSV News, March 27, 2023, https://www.osvnews.com/2023/03/27/polands-ulma-family-murdered-by-nazis-is-present-in-life-suffering-of-maryland-family/

"*Polonia: a Markowa museo dei polacchi che salvarono*

Ebrei," Ansa, March 17, 2016, https://www.ansa.it/nuova_europa/it/notizie/nazioni/polonia/2016/03/18/polonia-a-markowa-museo-dei-polacchi-che-salvarono-ebrei_083f999a-fe34-4b06-9d1f-9fb1c653edf7.html.

Sambucci, I., "*Gli Ulma presto beati, il postulatore: 'Una famiglia martire per amore,*'" Vatican News, December 21, 2022, https://www.vaticannews.va/it/chiesa/news/2022-12/famiglia-ulma-beati-intervista-postulatore-polonia.html.

Speech by Frank on the Extermination of the Jews, December 16, 1941, https://www.yadvashem.org/docs/frank-speech-on-jews-extermination.html.

Szulikowska, M. E., Interview with the Opoka portal, May 18, 2023, https://opoka.org.pl/News/Polska/2023/wiktoria-ulma-opowiesc-o-matczynej-milosci.

Other Sites:

heschel.kul.pl
kaplica-pamieci.pl
libguides.nypl.org/yizkorbooks
muzeumulmow.pl
ulmowie.pl

ABOUT THE AUTHORS

Fr. Paweł Rytel-Andrianik, a priest and professor at the Pontifical University of the Holy Cross in Rome, is editor-in-chief of the Polish Section of the Vatican Radio – Vatican News, and deputy director of the Abraham J. Heschel Center for Christian-Jewish Relations at the Catholic University of Lublin. The grandson of a prisoner in Treblinka I, he has written articles and books on imprisonment in concentration camps in World War II.

Manuela Tulli, from Rome, is a journalist covering the Vatican and religious topics for the Ansa news agency. Among her books is *Eroi della fede*, on the situation of Christians in the Middle East, and *Il grande tema del senso della vita* (*The Great Theme of the Meaning of Life*). At her blog *Fratello Cibo*, she writes about saints and cuisine. She is married and the mother of three children.